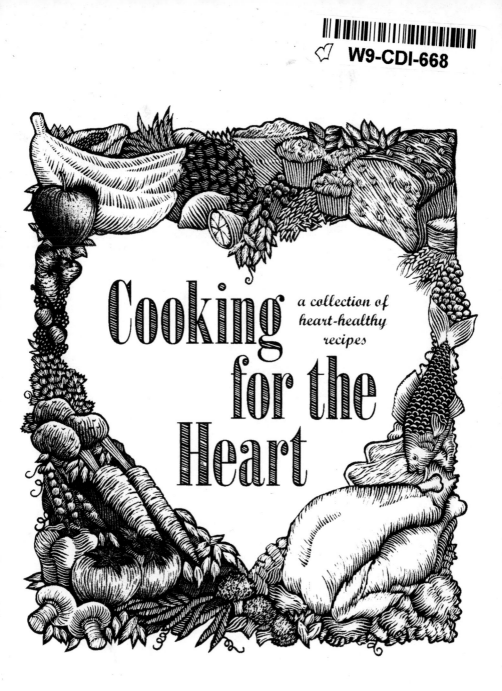

Cooking for the Heart

a collection of heart-healthy recipes

Nutritional analysis provided by Tammi Hancock, R.D., L.D.

Copyright ©1996

CPI
ASI 46499

THIS BOOK includes the finest plastic ring binders available, BUT, like most plastics, the BINDERS CAN BE DAMAGED BY EXCESSIVE HEAT, so AVOID exposing them to the direct rays of the SUN, or excessive heat such as IN A CAR on a hot day, or on the top of the kitchen STOVE. If not exposed to heat, the binders will last indefinitely.

ISBN #0-934474-78-8

Printed in the USA

Tammi Hancock is a consulting dietitian, registered with the American Dietetic Association and licensed in the state of Kansas. She worked for 7 years as a clinical dietitian in hospitals, including Mayo Medical Center in Rochester, Minnesota. She now runs her own business, providing nutrition services to cookbook authors and publishers and to health care institutions.

Suggestions for Lowering Fat Content in Your Diet

FOOD CATEGORY	CHOOSE	DECREASE
Meat Fish Poultry	Lean cuts of meat with fat trimmed, such as: beef-round, sirloin, rump steak, loin Poultry without skin Pork tenderloin	"Prime" grade meats Fatty cuts, like: corned beef, brisket, short ribs, spareribs Goose, duck, organ meats, sausage, bacon, hot dogs, regular luncheon meats
Dairy Products	Skim milk, lowfat buttermilk, lowfat evaporated or nonfat milk Lowfat or nonfat yogurts and cheeses	Whole milk, cream, half & half, nondairy creamers, real or nondairy whipped cream, cream cheese, sour cream, ice cream, custard-style yogurt High-fat cheese, like: Brie, Swiss, American, Cheddar
Eggs	Egg whites, cholesterol and fat-free egg substitutes	Egg yolks (substitute 2 egg whites for 1 egg)
Fats Oils	Unsaturated vegetable oils (in limited quantities): corn, olive, peanut, canola, safflower, sesame, soybean Fat-free mayonnaise, cream cheese, and salad dressings Mustard and flavored vinegars (Use spray oils or nonstick pans to help reduce fat content. Also, try substituting applesauce for fat in a recipe.)	Butter, coconut oil, palm kernel oil, palm oil, lard, bacon fat
Breads Cereals Pasta	Breads like whole wheat, pumpernickel, rye, pita, bagels, English muffins, rice cakes Lowfat crackers and bread sticks Plain cereals (hot and cold) Spaghetti and macaroni Any grain Dried peas and beans	Croissants, butter rolls, sweet rolls, pastries, doughnuts, most snack crackers, granola-type cereals made with saturated fats, egg noodles, pasta and rice prepared with cream, butter, or cheese sauces
Vegetables Fruits	Fresh, frozen, canned (no salt added)	Vegetables prepared in butter, cream, or sauce Fruits served in glazes

Fat Facts

Reducing fat in the diet is a major focus in America today, and for good reason. A high fat diet can contribute to elevated blood cholesterol levels, a risk factor for heart disease. Excess dietary fat has also been linked to obesity and cancer. As a result, lowering fat intake has become a priority for many.

Cholesterol is a fat-type substance found in all animal tissues. In adults, a blood cholesterol level below 200 milligrams per deciliter is desirable. A level above 240 milligrams is considered high. Blood cholesterol can also be broken into two categories: "good" and "bad" cholesterol. High density lipoproteins (HDL) are known as "good" cholesterol because of their high protein content and low cholesterol content, and because people with higher HDL levels have a lower incidence of heart disease. Low density lipoproteins (LDL) contain more cholesterol than HDL and are responsible for cholesterol build-up on artery walls, thus earning the label "bad" cholesterol. A low fat, low cholesterol diet, as well as exercise and being at a desirable weight, can help lower blood cholesterol levels and raise HDL levels.

Dietary fat can be divided into three different types: saturated, poly-unsaturated, and monounsaturated. Foods we eat contain a mixture of these fats.

- **SATURATED FATS** are generally solid at room temperature. They have been shown to increase blood cholesterol levels. Saturated fats are primarily found in animal products such as butter, milk, cream, and lard. Some plant foods, such as palm oil, coconut oil, vegetable shortening, and some peanut butters also contain large amounts of saturated fats.

- **POLYUNSATURATED FATS** tend to lower blood cholesterol levels. These fats are found in high concentrations in vegetable oils, and are usually liquid at room temperature. Fats such as sunflower oil, corn oil, and soft margarines have large amounts of polyunsaturated fats.

- **MONOUNSATURATED FATS** have also been shown to decrease cholesterol levels in the blood. They can be liquid or solid at room temperature, and can be from plant or animal sources. Olive, peanut, and canola oils are high in monounsaturated fats.

- **DIETARY CHOLESTEROL** comes from animal sources such as meat, poultry, fish and other seafood, and dairy products. Egg yolks and organ meats contain high amounts of dietary cholesterol.

- **HYDROGENATION** is a chemical process in which hydrogen is added to unsaturated oils to make them firmer at room temperature. Hydrogenated fats such as shortening or margarine are more saturated than the oil from which they are made. When choosing a margarine, pick one with 2 grams or less saturated fat per tablespoon.

Heart Healthy guidelines include: (1) Limit total fat intake to 30% or less of total calories. (2) Of these calories, up to one-third can be saturated fat, and the remaining two-thirds should come from polyunsaturated and monounsaturated sources. (3) Limit daily cholesterol intake to 300 milligrams or less.

Food Labeling Definitions

Government regulations give specific guidelines as to what words can be used on a food label to describe the product. Here is a list of these descriptive terms.

FREE A product must contain no amount or only an insignificant amount of one or more of the following: fat, saturated fat, cholesterol, sodium, sugar, and calories. The terms *no, without,* and *zero* can also be used.

Calorie-free: less than 5 calories per serving
Sugar-free or Fat-free: less than 0.5g per serving
Sodium-free: less than 5mg per serving

LOW This term can be used when referring to one or more of the following: fat, cholesterol, sodium, and calories. The terms *little, few,* and *low source of* can also be used.

Low calorie: 40 calories or less per serving
Low fat: 3g or less per serving
Low saturated fat: 1g or less per serving
Low cholesterol: less than 20mg per serving
Low sodium: less than 140mg per serving
Very low sodium: less than 35mg per serving

LEAN Meat, poultry, and seafood containing less than 10g of fat, less than 4g saturated fat, and less than 95mg of cholesterol per 3.5 oz. serving.

EXTRA LEAN Meat, poultry, and seafood containing less than 5g of fat, less than 2g saturated fat, and less than 95mg of cholesterol per 3.5 oz. serving.

HIGH One serving of a product must contain 20% or more of the *Daily Value* (recommended daily intake of a nutrient).

GOOD SOURCE One serving must contain 10% to 19% of the Daily Value.

REDUCED A nutritionally altered product containing 25% less of a nutrient or of calories than the regular product. If the regular product already meets the criteria for *low, a reduced* claim cannot be made.

LESS A food that contains 25% less of a nutrient or of calories than a similar food. Cream cheeses that have 25% less fat than butter could use the term *less* or *fewer.*

LIGHT This term can still be used to describe food characteristics such as color and texture if the label makes the meaning clear; for example, *light brown sugar.*
The term also carries two other meanings:

+ A nutritionally altered product that contains one-third less calories or half the fat of the original food
+ A food's sodium content has been cut by 50% or more

MORE A food using this claim must contain 10% more of the Daily Value of a nutrient than the reference food. To use the words *fortified, enriched,* or *added,* this standard must also be met.

UNSALTED, NO SALT ADDED, or WITHOUT ADDED SALT The sodium naturally found in the product is still there, but it has been prepared without the salt that is normally added.

Sodium

Sodium is a mineral used by the body to maintain a proper balance of water in the blood. Although it is a vital nutrient, the body needs very little sodium to stay healthy. Because it is found naturally in some foods and is added to many other foods, getting too little sodium is usually not a problem. A high sodium diet, on the other hand, can contribute to high blood pressure in some people. Reducing sodium intake in the diet may help prevent or control high blood pressure. It is hard to know who will develop high blood pressure, or who might benefit from eating less sodium. For these reasons, and because most individuals consume much more sodium than needed, it is generally suggested that we reduce sodium intake.

Table salt is the major source of sodium in our diet. It is made up of about half sodium and half chloride. An adult diet containing between 1,100mg and 3,300mg of sodium per day is considered adequate. One teaspoon of salt contains 2,000mg of sodium.

WAYS TO REDUCE DIETARY SODIUM

✦ Taste food before salting. Salt food only sparingly at the table.

✦ Cut back on sodium slowly to give the body time to adjust to less salty flavors. *Salt-craving* taste buds will eventually be replaced by new ones that do not have an affinity for salt.

✦ Choose foods that have little or no sodium added. In general, the more processed the food, the more sodium it contains. For example, processed turkey breast purchased at a deli has considerably more sodium than fresh turkey breast.

✦ In many recipes, the salt can be cut back or even eliminated without greatly affecting the taste. Experiment with recipes at home, using less salt each time and using low sodium substitutes for high sodium ingredients.

✦ Read labels on food packages. Compare the sodium content to similar items and to the recommended sodium intake for an entire day.

✦ Limit intake of high sodium foods such as cheeses, processed meats, soups, broths, snack foods, canned vegetables and vegetable juices, pickled vegetables, gravies, sauces, commercial casserole mixes, frozen dinners, and condiments. In many cases, lower sodium alternatives are available.

✦ When eating in restaurants, ask for foods to be prepared without added salt and request to have sauces, gravies, dressings, and condiments served on the side.

✦ Use herbs and spices instead of salt to enhance the flavor of foods. Check the label of seasonings to be sure they do not contain sodium. Use onion powder rather than onion salt, garlic powder instead of garlic salt. In place of seasoning salt, try commercially prepared herb and spice blends or make your own.

TABLE OF CONTENTS

"Heart Healthy" Recipe Substitutions

ORIGINAL INGREDIENT	ALTERNATIVE	REDUCES:		
		TF	SF	C
1 pound ground beef	• 1 pound ground turkey	✔	✔	✔
1 ounce Cheddar, Swiss, or American cheese	• 1 ounce lowfat cheese • 1 ounce part-skim cheese (Mozzarella)	✔ ✔	✔ ✔	✔ ✔
1 egg	• 2 egg whites • ¼ c. low cholesterol egg substitute	✔ ✔	✔ ✔	✔ ✔
1 c. whole milk	• 1 c. skim milk	✔	✔	✔
1 c. cream	• 1 c. evaporated skim milk	✔	✔	✔
1 c. sour cream	• 1 c. nonfat sour cream • 1 c. plain nonfat yogurt • 1 c. lowfat cottage cheese plus 1 to 2 tsp. lemon juice, blended smooth	✔ ✔ ✔	✔ ✔ ✔	✔ ✔ ✔
1 ounce cream cheese	• 1 ounce nonfat cream cheese • 1 ounce Neufchatel cheese	✔ ✔	✔ ✔	✔ ✔
1 c. butter	• 1 c. margarine • 1 c. vegetable oil		✔ ✔	✔ ✔
1 c. shortening	• 7 fluid oz. vegetable oil		✔	
1 ounce baking chocolate	• 3 Tbsp. cocoa powder plus 1 Tbsp. vegetable oil		✔	
roux: 1 part fat 1 part starch	• ½ part fat to 1 part starch	✔		
1 can condensed cream soup	• Mix together: ½ c. nonfat dry milk 2 Tbsp. cornstarch 2 tsp. low sodium chicken bouillon ¼ tsp. onion powder ⅛ tsp. garlic powder ¼ tsp. basil ¼ tsp. thyme ¼ tsp. white pepper 9 oz. cold water Add the following if desired: ¼ c. chopped celery or ½ c. sliced mushrooms Heat to a boil; stir frequently. Per "can": 215 calories, 1g fat, 8mg cholesterol, 200mg sodium	✔	✔	✔

KEY:
TF = total fat
SF = saturated fat
C = cholesterol

APPETIZERS, BEVERAGES

BAKED POTATO SKINS

6 large baking potatoes
2½ Tbsp. butter or
margarine, melted
1¼ tsp. freshly ground
pepper
½ tsp. onion salt
½ tsp. garlic salt
¼ c. grated Parmesan
cheese
Mock sour cream

Scrub potatoes thoroughly and prick several times with a fork. Bake at 400° for 1 to 1¼ hours or until done. Allow to cool to touch. Cut potatoes in halves lengthwise; carefully scoop out pulp, leaving about ¼ inch thick shells (reserve pulp for other uses). Cut each shell into 1 inch wide strips and place on ungreased baking sheets. Brush tops of strips with butter; sprinkle with seasonings and cheese. Bake at 400° for 10 to 12 minutes or until crisp; serve warm with sour cream. Makes 3 dozen.

NUTRITIONAL INFORMATION

Calories	30	Sat. Fat (grams)	0.6 g
Total Fat	1 g	Cholesterol (mg)	3 mg
% Fat	30	Sodium (mg)	59 mg

Above figures based on per serving basis.

MOCK SOUR CREAM

¾ c. lowfat cottage
cheese
¼ c. nonfat plain yogurt
½ tsp. lemon juice
1 packet Equal artificial
sweetener

Mix well. Refrigerate and serve. Makes 16 servings.

NUTRITIONAL INFORMATION

Calories	10	Sat. Fat (grams)	0 g
Total Fat	less than 1 g	Cholesterol (mg)	1 mg
% Fat	11	Sodium (mg)	50 mg

Above figures based on 1 tablespoon serving.

CHEESE-STUFFED CELERY APPETIZER

¼ c. minced celery
¼ c. scallions (green
   onions)
4 oz. fat free extra sharp
   Cheddar cheese,
   shredded
1 tsp. Dijon style
   mustard
Dash of garlic powder
Dash of Worcestershire
   sauce
½ c. plain lowfat yogurt
8 medium celery ribs

Spray top half of double boiler with nonstick cooking spray; add celery and scallions. Cover and cook directly over low heat until celery is tender, stirring occasionally to prevent sticking or burning. Place over hot water and add cheese, mustard, garlic powder, and Worcestershire sauce to vegetable mixture. Cook, stirring constantly, until cheese is melted.

Spoon yogurt into a bowl and, using a wire whisk, gradually stir in cheese mixture, stirring until thoroughly blended; cover and refrigerate until firm.

To serve: Fill each celery rib with ⅛ of the cheese mixture. Makes 8 servings.

NUTRITIONAL INFORMATION	
Calories.................40	Sat. Fat (grams).........0 g
Total Fat......less than 1 g	Cholesterol (mg).........2 mg
% Fat......................8	Sodium (mg)..........173 mg

Above figures based on per serving basis.

CHICKEN SPREAD

1½ lb. skinless chicken
   breasts
8 oz. fat free cream
   cheese, softened
1 Tbsp. grated onion
1 Tbsp. lowfat
   mayonnaise
1 Tbsp. sweet pickle
   juice
½ c. finely chopped
   celery
Dash of curry powder
¼ tsp. salt
¼ tsp. pepper
½ Tbsp. chopped
   pimento
Dash of hot sauce
Dash of garlic powder

Cook chicken till tender. Remove from broth, reserving 2 tablespoons broth. Cool. Bone chicken and chop fine; set aside.

Combine the cream cheese and mayonnaise, beating till smooth; add remaining ingredients and mix well. Stir in chicken and reserved chicken broth. Lightly coat desired mold with cooking spray; press in chicken mixture and chill.

Unmold on lettuce lined serving plate; garnish with olives and radishes. Serve with Melba toast. Makes 2 dozen.

NUTRITIONAL INFORMATION	
Calories.................43	Sat. Fat (grams).........0 g
Total Fat......less than 1 g	Cholesterol (mg).......17 mg
% Fat......................11	Sodium (mg)...........98 mg

Above figures based on per serving basis.

CHILI SAUCE DIP

1 (12 oz.) bottle chili
  sauce
2 Tbsp. horseradish
3 to 4 drops of Tabasco
  sauce
2 Tbsp. lemon juice
¼ c. finely chopped
  celery
¼ tsp. salt
1 Tbsp. minced parsley

Combine ingredients. Chill and serve with crisp raw vegetables. Makes 24 (1 tablespoon) servings.

NUTRITIONAL INFORMATION	
Calories.................16	Sat. Fat (grams)..........0 g
Total Fat......less than 1 g	Cholesterol (mg).........0 mg
% Fat......................3	Sodium (mg)..........215 mg

Above figures based on per serving basis.

ORIENTAL CHICKEN WINGS

2½ c. low sodium soy
  sauce
3 c. sugar
4 or 5 slices ginger root
4 or 5 cloves garlic,
  pounded
2 green onions, chopped
1 large pkg. skinless
  chicken wings

Mix soy sauce, sugar, ginger root, garlic, and green onions. Stir till sugar is dissolved. (This will take awhile.) Cut chicken wings in pieces; throw tips away or use for making chicken broth. Marinate wings for 3 days. Bake in marinade for 35 to 40 minutes at 350°. Makes 10 (4 piece) servings.

NUTRITIONAL INFORMATION	
Calories.................149	Sat. Fat (grams).......0.6 g
Total Fat...................2 g	Cholesterol (mg).......34 mg
% Fat......................13	Sodium (mg)..........554 mg

Above figures based on per serving basis.

BUFFALO WINGS

2 lb. fresh skinless
  chicken wings,
  disjointed
1 c. Tabasco (hot pepper)
  sauce
1 c. tomato juice

Separate chicken wings and wash thoroughly. Roast at 400° for 30 to 45 minutes until golden, turning once if necessary, for even browning. Prepare 2 bowls of sauce: One of straight Tabasco sauce for *hot* wings and 1 of half Tabasco/half tomato juice for medium hot wings. When wings are hot and crisp, submerge, a few at a time, into bowls of sauce. Leave for 1 minute to absorb flavors. Remove with a slotted spoon and return to oven to further crisp and brown. The wings are usually served with celery sticks, Blue cheese dressing for dipping, and plenty of cold drinks. Makes 5 (4 piece) servings.

NUTRITIONAL INFORMATION

Calories	83	Sat. Fat (grams)	0.6 g
Total Fat	2 g	Cholesterol (mg)	34 mg
% Fat	26	Sodium (mg)	285 mg

Above figures based on per serving basis.

CUCUMBER AND YOGURT DIP

1 cucumber
1 (8 oz.) container plain
  lowfat yogurt
Garlic powder to taste
¼ tsp. Worcestershire
  sauce

Scrub cucumber if using fresh garden cucumbers; otherwise, peel cucumber. Grate cucumber in a food processor and drain very well, until almost dry. Combine with other ingredients and serve with fresh veggies or crackers. Makes 24 (1 tablespoon) servings.

NUTRITIONAL INFORMATION

Calories	8	Sat. Fat (grams)	0 g
Total Fat	less than 1 g	Cholesterol (mg)	1 mg
% Fat	19	Sodium (mg)	7 mg

Above figures based on per serving basis.

CRABMEAT SUPREME ON CELERY STICKS

½ lb. crabmeat
4 Tbsp. fat free salad
  dressing
15 walnut halves,
  chopped
1 tsp. low salt sweet
  relish

Mix together crabmeat, salad dressing, walnuts, and sweet relish. Fill celery stick with mixture. Makes 18 celery sticks.

NUTRITIONAL INFORMATION	
Calories...................55	Sat. Fat (grams)..........0 g
Total Fat...................2 g	Cholesterol (mg).......38 mg
% Fat.....................29	Sodium (mg)..........145 mg

Above figures based on per serving basis.

FRUIT-NUT SNACK MIX

¾ c. dried apricots, cut
  in quarters
¾ c. dates, cut in halves
¾ c. raisins
3 Tbsp. whole almonds
¼ c. walnut halves
¼ c. unsalted peanuts
⅛ c. unsalted sunflower
  seeds

Toss ingredients together. Store in tightly covered container. You may add your favorite dried fruits or nuts in place of those listed. Makes 8 (⅓ cup) servings.

NUTRITIONAL INFORMATION	
Calories.................200	Sat. Fat (grams).......0.8 g
Total Fat...................7 g	Cholesterol (mg).........0 mg
% Fat.....................30	Sodium (mg)..............5 mg

Above figures based on per serving basis.

GARDEN VEGETABLE DIP

1 (8 or 9 oz.) container
  cottage cheese
2 Tbsp. skim milk
1 Tbsp. finely chopped
  green peppers
1 Tbsp. finely chopped
  onions
1 Tbsp. finely chopped
  radish
¼ tsp. celery salt
Sprinkle of salt and
  pepper

Blend cottage cheese and milk until creamy. Stir in remaining ingredients. Chill for 1 hour or more. Serve with crisp, cold vegetables. Makes 20 (1 tablespoon) servings.

NUTRITIONAL INFORMATION	
Calories...................11	Sat. Fat (grams)..........0 g
Total Fat......less than 1 g	Cholesterol (mg).........1 mg
% Fat.....................19	Sodium (mg)..........63 mg

Above figures based on per serving basis.

HEART HEALTHY MUNCH MIX

2 Tbsp. low calorie
  margarine
¼ c. honey
1 Tbsp. lemon peel,
  grated
¼ tsp. cinnamon
2 qt. air-popped popcorn
  (plain)
1 c. raisins
1½ c. dried apricots,
  chopped
1 c. dry roasted unsalted
  peanuts

In a small saucepan, melt margarine; stir in honey, lemon peel, and cinnamon. Drizzle over popcorn in large bowl. Add raisins, apricots, and peanuts. Toss gently until well mixed. Makes 10 (½ cup) servings.

NUTRITIONAL INFORMATION			
Calories	242	Sat. Fat (grams)	1.3 g
Total Fat	9 g	Cholesterol (mg)	0 mg
% Fat	30	Sodium (mg)	15 mg

Above figures based on per serving basis.

HEART HEALTHY SPINACH DIP

1 (10 oz.) pkg. frozen
  chopped spinach
1 pkg. Knorr vegetable
  soup and recipe mix
1¼ c. light sour cream
1 c. fat free mayonnaise
1 (8 oz.) can water
  chestnuts, chopped
3 green onions, chopped

Thaw spinach and squeeze dry. Stir soup mix, sour cream, and mayonnaise until blended. Stir in spinach, water chestnuts, and green onions. Cover and chill for 2 hours. Stir before serving. Makes 4 cups, 1 tablespoon per serving.

NUTRITIONAL INFORMATION			
Calories	13	Sat. Fat (grams)	0.3 g
Total Fat	less than 1 g	Cholesterol (mg)	2 mg
% Fat	30	Sodium (mg)	79 mg

Above figures based on per serving basis.

SPINACH-STUFFED MUSHROOMS

1½ lb. fresh mushrooms
2 tsp. butter or
  margarine, melted
1 (10 oz.) pkg. frozen
  chopped spinach
¼ c. minced onion
¼ c. minced celery
1 clove garlic, minced
1 (4 oz.) jar diced
  pimiento, drained
1 tsp. Worcestershire
  sauce
¼ tsp. salt
¼ tsp. pepper
2 Tbsp. grated Parmesan
  cheese

Clean mushrooms with damp paper towels. Remove mushroom stems and finely chop; set aside. Brush caps with butter and set aside.

Cook spinach according to package directions; drain well and squeeze out excess liquid. Set aside.

Saute mushroom stems, onion, celery, and garlic in non-stick pan sprayed with cooking spray until tender. Remove from heat; add spinach, pimiento, Worcestershire sauce, salt, and pepper, mixing well. Spoon mixture into mushroom caps. Place on a lightly greased baking sheet; sprinkle with cheese. Bake mushrooms at 350° for 10 to 15 minutes. Makes about 2 dozen.

NUTRITIONAL INFORMATION

Calories	17	Sat. Fat (grams)	0.3 g
Total Fat	1 g	Cholesterol (mg)	1 mg
% Fat	29	Sodium (mg)	49 mg

Above figures based on per serving basis.

ZESTY MUSHROOM CAPS

1½ lb. large fresh
  mushrooms
6 oz. skinless white
  turkey meat, ground
3 Tbsp. finely chopped
  sweet red pepper
¾ c. finely shredded
  part-skim milk cheese
¼ c. bread crumbs
2 Tbsp. minced fresh or
  dried parsley flakes

Remove stem from mushrooms. Wipe caps with damp cloth. Finely chop stems and add to ground turkey meat. In a skillet, saute chopped mushroom stems, turkey meat, and red pepper for 10 minutes.

In a large bowl, combine turkey mixture, ½ cup shredded cheese, bread crumbs, and parsley. Generously fill mushroom caps with turkey filling. Place on 15½ x 10½ inch jelly roll pan. Bake in preheated oven (400°) for 8 to 10 minutes. Remove from oven; sprinkle with remaining cheese. Serve warm. Makes 30 mushrooms.

NUTRITIONAL INFORMATION

Calories	23	Sat. Fat (grams)	0.3 g
Total Fat	1 g	Cholesterol (mg)	5 mg
% Fat	25	Sodium (mg)	24 mg

Above figures based on per serving basis.

PINTO BEAN DIP

1 onion, chopped
2 cloves garlic, minced
1 Tbsp. safflower oil
1 green chili pepper, chopped
½ tsp. cumin
1 tsp. chili powder
1½ c. cooked, drained pinto beans (or substitute kidney or black beans)
¼ c. chopped cilantro
¼ c. natural picante sauce

Saute onion and garlic in oil until onion is transparent. Add chili pepper and cook until soft. Transfer mixture to food processor. Add remaining ingredients and process until smooth. Serve chilled or at room temperature with corn chips, raw vegetables, whole wheat tortillas, or as a sandwich spread. Makes about 2 cups, 1 tablespoon per serving.

NUTRITIONAL INFORMATION	
Calories...................18	Sat. Fat (grams).........0 g
Total Fat......less than 1 g	Cholesterol (mg).........0 mg
% Fat.....................24	Sodium (mg)............14 mg

Above figures based on per serving basis.

SALMON SPREAD

½ c. finely chopped celery
1 green onion, thinly sliced
1 Tbsp. water
4 oz. fat free cream cheese
1 (6¾ oz.) can red salmon, drained
1 tsp. dill weed
1 tsp. lemon juice
¼ tsp. garlic salt
Dash of pepper

1. Combine celery, onion, and water in 2 cup microwave-safe measure.
2. Microwave (HIGH), uncovered, for 1½ to 2 minutes or until tender. Add cheese.
3. Microwave (HIGH), uncovered, for 30 to 45 seconds or until cheese is softened. Mix in salmon, dill weed, lemon juice, garlic salt, and pepper. Place in serving bowl. Cover and refrigerate until served. If desired, garnish with snipped fresh parsley or dill. Makes about 1½ cups, 2 tablespoons per serving.

Enjoy this spread on crackers or bread, or thin with skim milk and use as a dip for fresh vegetables.

NUTRITIONAL INFORMATION	
Calories...................27	Sat. Fat (grams).........0 g
Total Fat...................1 g	Cholesterol (mg).........5 mg
% Fat.....................27	Sodium (mg)..........123 mg

Above figures based on per serving basis.

TUNA STUFFED TOMATOES

1 (6½ oz.) can chunk
 light tuna (in water)
½ c. chopped celery
⅓ c. low-cal mayonnaise-
 type salad dressing
¼ c. chopped parsley
2 Tbsp. minced onion
¼ tsp. black pepper
36 cherry tomatoes

Drain tuna; combine tuna, celery, mayonnaise, chopped parsley, green onion, and pepper. Cut tops off tomatoes and scoop out seeds. Turn upside down to drain. Fill with tuna salad. Serve chilled. Makes 36 appetizers.

NUTRITIONAL INFORMATION	
Calories...................14	Sat. Fat (grams)..........0 g
Total Fat......less than 1 g	Cholesterol (mg)..........2 mg
% Fat.....................30	Sodium (mg)..............31 mg

Above figures based on per serving basis.

TURKEY MEATBALLS

1 lb. skinless white
 turkey meat, ground
2 slices white bread,
 diced
½ c. dry bread crumbs
¼ c. grated Romano
 cheese
2 egg whites
½ celery rib, finely
 chopped
1 very small onion,
 chopped
½ tsp. oregano
½ tsp. basil

Mix all ingredients well in food processor or by hand. Shape into small balls. Bake on lightly greased cookie sheet at 350° for 30 minutes. Serve with toothpicks. Makes 24 meatballs.

NUTRITIONAL INFORMATION	
Calories...................44	Sat. Fat (grams).......0.3 g
Total Fat....................1 g	Cholesterol (mg).......14 mg
% Fat.....................15	Sodium (mg)..............58 mg

Above figures based on per serving basis.

VEGETABLE SANDWICH

1 c. celery, diced
1 onion, diced
2 small carrots, grated
1 small cucumber, diced
½ green pepper
1 tsp. salt
2 c. fat free mayonnaise
1 env. unflavored gelatin

Soak gelatin in a little water, then melt over hot water. Mix all ingredients and add gelatin. Put in refrigerator to cool. Spread on bread and cut into desired sizes. Wrap in foil and keep in refrigerator. Will keep for 2 to 3 days. Makes 16 (¼ cup) servings.

NUTRITIONAL INFORMATION	
Calories...................32	Sat. Fat (grams)..........0 g
Total Fat......less than 1 g	Cholesterol (mg).........0 mg
% Fat......................2	Sodium (mg)..........354 mg

Above figures based on per serving basis.

BANANA SLUSH PUNCH

3 qt. water
3 c. sugar
6 to 8 mashed bananas
2 small cans orange juice
(frozen concentrate)
3 small cans lemonade
(frozen concentrate)
1 large can pineapple
juice
3 qt. ginger ale

Heat water and sugar until sugar dissolves, stirring constantly; cool. Add all other ingredients in a large bowl; stir. Freeze in containers.

When ready to serve, take out a container of punch and pour ginger ale on top, a little at a time, and break up with potato masher until slushy. Serve in punch bowl. Makes 36 (1 cup) servings.

NUTRITIONAL INFORMATION

Calories	187	Sat. Fat (grams)	0 g
Total Fat	less than 1 g	Cholesterol (mg)	0 mg
% Fat	1	Sodium (mg)	8 mg

Above figures based on per serving basis.

BLACK COW

1 c. diet root beer
3 oz. vanilla sugar free,
fat free frozen dessert
1 Tbsp. prepared low
calorie whipped
topping mix

Chill a tall glass. Into chilled glass, pour root beer; scoop vanilla frozen dessert into glass and top with low calorie whipped topping mix. Serve with a straw and long handled spoon. Serves 1.

NUTRITIONAL INFORMATION

Calories	65	Sat. Fat (grams)	0.8 g
Total Fat	1 g	Cholesterol (mg)	2 mg
% Fat	12	Sodium (mg)	90 mg

Above figures based on per serving basis.

BREAKFAST IN A GLASS

1 medium banana
¼ c. pasteurized egg
substitute
⅓ c. water
1½ Tbsp. frozen orange
concentrate
1 tsp. wheat germ
1 tsp. honey

Slice banana into blender. Add all remaining ingredients and blend at high speed for 1 minute. Serves 1.

NUTRITIONAL INFORMATION

Calories	251	Sat. Fat (grams)	1.8 g
Total Fat	6 g	Cholesterol (mg)	213 mg
% Fat	20	Sodium (mg)	65 mg

Above figures based on per serving basis.

BREAKFAST SMOOTHIE

1 large ripe banana,
  peeled and frozen
1 c. fresh pineapple
  chunks (may use lite
  can chunks)
1 c. strawberries (fresh
  or frozen)
1 (8 oz.) ctn. low calorie
  strawberry yogurt

Slice frozen banana into blender. Add remaining ingredients to blender. Whip until pureed. Serves 2.

NUTRITIONAL INFORMATION	
Calories.................237	Sat. Fat (grams).......0.9 g
Total Fat...................2 g	Cholesterol (mg).........7 mg
% Fat.......................8	Sodium (mg)............57 mg

Above figures based on per serving basis.

FLORIDA FREEZE

½ c. orange juice
¼ c. grapefruit juice
½ c. pineapple chunks
½ medium banana

Place ingredients in a blender. Mix until creamy. Serve over crushed ice. Serves 2.

NUTRITIONAL INFORMATION	
Calories.................86	Sat. Fat (grams).........0 g
Total Fat......less than 1 g	Cholesterol (mg).........0 mg
% Fat.......................4	Sodium (mg)..............2 mg

Above figures based on per serving basis.

FROSTED PEACH

1 medium peach, peeled,
  pitted, and quartered
½ c. fat free plain yogurt
¼ c. pasteurized egg
  substitute
Sugar substitute to equal
  2 tsp. sugar (or to
  taste)
¼ tsp. ground cinnamon
⅛ tsp. lemon extract
2 to 3 ice cubes

In blender, process all ingredients until smooth. Serves 1.

NUTRITIONAL INFORMATION	
Calories.................191	Sat. Fat (grams).......1.7 g
Total Fat...................5 g	Cholesterol (mg).....215 mg
% Fat.......................25	Sodium (mg)..........157 mg

Above figures based on per serving basis.

FROSTY ORANGE AUTUMN DRINK

½ c. orange juice
¼ c. frozen pasteurized
egg substitute, thawed
3 Tbsp. nonfat dry milk
powder
Noncalorie sweetener to
equal 4 tsp. sugar
4 to 5 ice cubes

In blender, combine all ingredients, except ice. Blend until smooth. Add ice cubes, one at a time. Serves 1.

NUTRITIONAL INFORMATION

Calories.................213	Sat. Fat (grams).......1.2 g
Total Fat...................7 g	Cholesterol (mg)........4 mg
% Fat.....................29	Sodium (mg)..........192 mg

Above figures based on per serving basis.

MIAMI LIME LIFT

2 fresh Florida limes
½ c. sugar or sugar
substitute
1 qt. boiling water
Lime slices for garnish

Slice limes thinly. Put in bowl with sugar. Let stand for 1 hour. Pour boiling water into bowl. Cool, then chill. To serve, pour limeade and several lime slices over ice in tall glasses. Hang a lime slice over edge of glass. Serve with long straw. Makes 1 quart, 4 (1 cup) servings.

NUTRITIONAL INFORMATION

Calories.................107	Sat. Fat (grams).........0 g
Total Fat......less than 1 g	Cholesterol (mg)........0 mg
% Fat.....................1	Sodium (mg)..............1 mg

Above figures based on per serving basis.

MANGO ISLAND SHAKE

1 mango
½ c. orange juice
½ c. vanilla yogurt
4 ice cubes

Peel and slice mango. Place all ingredients in blender. Blend and serve. Serves 1 or 2 (depends on size of glass).

NUTRITIONAL INFORMATION

Calories.................314	Sat. Fat (grams).......2.6 g
Total Fat...................5 g	Cholesterol (mg).......12 mg
% Fat.....................12	Sodium (mg)..........84 mg

Above figures based on per serving basis.

PINEAPPLE OR STRAWBERRY SHAKES

1 c. skim or nonfat milk
½ c. canned crushed
  pineapple (no sugar
  added), chilled*
½ tsp. coconut or rum
  extract
Granulated sugar
  substitute to taste
  (optional)

In blender container, combine milk, pineapple, extract, and, if desired, sugar substitute; process until smooth. Serves 1.

*One cup chilled strawberries may be substituted.

NUTRITIONAL INFORMATION	
Calories................169	Sat. Fat (grams).......0.3 g
Total Fat...................1 g	Cholesterol (mg).........4 mg
% Fat........................3	Sodium (mg)..........128 mg

Above figures based on per serving basis.

PINK COW

1 c. low-cal raspberry
  yogurt
1 c. skim milk
1 fresh peach, peeled
  and sliced
1 packet sweetener
  (Equal or Sugar Twin)

Blend together thoroughly and serve chilled. Serves 2.

NUTRITIONAL INFORMATION	
Calories................181	Sat. Fat (grams).......1.1 g
Total Fat...................1 g	Cholesterol (mg).......11 mg
% Fat........................6	Sodium (mg)..........122 mg

Above figures based on per serving basis.

STRAWBERRY-BANANA SHAKE

2 c. fresh strawberries
2 c. nonfat buttermilk
1 small ripe banana,
  sliced (½ c.)
3 Tbsp. honey

Wash and cap strawberries; drain well. Place a single layer of strawberries in a shallow pan; freeze. Combine remaining ingredients in container of an electric blender. Process until smooth; slowly add frozen strawberries. Process until smooth. Serve immediately. Makes 4½ cups, 4 servings.

NUTRITIONAL INFORMATION	
Calories................146	Sat. Fat (grams).......0.7 g
Total Fat...................1 g	Cholesterol (mg).........4 mg
% Fat........................9	Sodium (mg)..........130 mg

Above figures based on per serving basis.

STRAWBERRY MINT LEMONADE

¼ c. fresh squeezed
lemon juice
½ c. fresh or frozen
strawberries
3 Tbsp. honey
3 c. water
1 (3 inch) mint sprig with
leaves

Combine strawberries and mint in blender container. Liquefy. Add honey and lemon. Process until smooth. Combine with water and ice cubes in a large glass bottle or pitcher. Makes 4 (1 cup) servings.

NUTRITIONAL INFORMATION	
Calories...................59	Sat. Fat (grams)..........0 g
Total Fat......less than 1 g	Cholesterol (mg).........0 mg
% Fat.......................1	Sodium (mg) ....3 mg

Above figures based on per serving basis.

SUNBURST PUNCH

½ c. lemon juice
3½ c. chilled pure
orange juice (not from
concentrate)
1 (46 oz.) can chilled
pineapple juice
2 (32 oz.) bottles ginger
ale
1 qt. orange pineapple,
lemon, or lime sherbet,
scooped in balls

Combine juices in large punch bowl, mixing well. Before ready to serve, add ginger ale and sherbet. Makes 35 (½ cup) servings.

NUTRITIONAL INFORMATION	
Calories...................84	Sat. Fat (grams).......0.3 g
Total Fat...................1 g	Cholesterol (mg).........1 mg
% Fat.......................5	Sodium (mg) ....15 mg

Above figures based on per serving basis.

TANGY-TART DRINK

1 pt. pure grapefruit
juice
1 pt. grape juice
1 qt. sugar free 7-Up or
ginger ale

Combine chilled juices and 7-Up or ginger ale. Add ice cubes. Makes 8 (1 cup) servings.

NUTRITIONAL INFORMATION	
Calories...................56	Sat. Fat (grams)..........0 g
Total Fat......less than 1 g	Cholesterol (mg).........0 mg
% Fat.......................2	Sodium (mg) ....35 mg

Above figures based on per serving basis.

SOUPS, SALADS, VEGETABLES

BLACK-EYED PEA SOUP WITH CORN BREAD DUMPLINGS

Soup:
2½ c. dried black-eyed
  peas (or 6 c. cooked)
6 c. water
3 large onions, sliced
  thin
6 garlic cloves, minced
1 c. minced celery
1 (28 oz.) can tomatoes
1 (6 oz.) can tomato
  paste
1 bunch fresh parsley,
  chopped
Salt and freshly ground
  pepper to taste

Dumplings:
1 c. corn meal
¼ c. whole wheat flour
2 tsp. baking powder
½ tsp. salt
2 egg whites, lightly
  beaten
½ c. soy milk or skim
  milk

To make soup: Sort and rinse the peas and soak them overnight in water twice their bulk. Drain and rinse the peas again and place them in a large Dutch oven with the water, onions, garlic, and celery, adding additional water to cover if necessary. Bring to a boil; reduce heat. Simmer until peas and vegetables are tender, about 45 minutes to 1 hour. Add the tomatoes and tomato paste. Continue to simmer for about 15 minutes. Add parsley, salt, and pepper. If dumplings are used, they may be added to the soup pot at this point or may be placed in individual serving bowls and the soup ladled over them. Serves 8.

To make dumplings: Preheat oven to 375°. Combine all ingredients in a large mixing bowl. Drop the batter by spoonfuls onto a greased cookie sheet. Bake for 13 to 15 minutes, until browned. Makes 16 dumplings, 2 per serving.

This soup freezes well. Dumplings may be frozen separately or in the soup.

NUTRITIONAL INFORMATION			
Calories	329	Sat. Fat (grams)	0.4 g
Total Fat	2 g	Cholesterol (mg)	0 mg
% Fat	4	Sodium (mg)	635 mg

Above figures based on per serving basis.

CHICKEN GUMBO SOUP

1 lb. cooked chicken, cut
  in small pieces
5 c. chicken broth
½ c. chopped onion
2 tsp. oil
½ c. chopped green
  peppers
1 c. cooked okra
1 c. cooked rice
1½ c. canned tomatoes
¾ c. canned corn
1 Tbsp. soy sauce
Salt and pepper to taste

Saute onions in oil for 5 minutes. Add all other ingredients. Bring to a boil. Simmer for 45 minutes to 1 hour. Contains approximately 95 calories per serving. Serves 10.

NUTRITIONAL INFORMATION	
Calories..................160	Sat. Fat (grams).......1.3 g
Total Fat....................5 g	Cholesterol (mg)......40mg
% Fat.....................30	Sodium (mg)..........658mg

Above figures based on per serving basis.

CHICKEN VEGETABLE SOUP

1 bay leaf
2½ qt. water
1 chicken, skinned
1 potato, diced
2 carrots, cut up
3 stalks celery, cut up
1 medium onion, cut up
½ tsp. Mrs. Dash

Boil cut up chicken in water for ¾ hour. Set to cool overnight. Boil vegetables till nearly done. Refrigerate till next day. Next day, take fat off top of chicken. Debone chicken and add several pieces to the broth. (Remove bay leaf after cooking the chicken.) Add vegetables and about ½ teaspoon of salt free Mrs. Dash. Boil together until vegetables soften. Serve with salt free crackers. Makes 12 (1 cup) servings.

One-half cup cooked rice may be added if desired. Rest of chicken can be used in salads or sandwiches.

NUTRITIONAL INFORMATION	
Calories..................54	Sat. Fat (grams)..........0 g
Total Fat....................1 g	Cholesterol (mg).......19mg
% Fat.....................15	Sodium (mg)..........35mg

Above figures based on per serving basis.

HEARTY PEA SOUP

2 Tbsp. oil
1 onion, diced
1 bay leaf
1 tsp. celery seed
1 c. split peas
¼ c. barley
½ c. lima beans
2 qt. water
2 tsp. salt
Dash of pepper
1 carrot, chopped
3 stalks celery, chopped
½ c. parsley, chopped
1 potato, diced
½ tsp. basil
½ tsp. thyme

Saute onion, bay leaf, and celery seed in oil. Add peas, barley, lima beans, and water; simmer for 1½ hours. Add salt, pepper, carrot, celery, parsley, potato, basil, and thyme; simmer for 30 to 45 minutes longer. Makes about 8 or 9 cups of soup.

NUTRITIONAL INFORMATION

Calories	203	Sat. Fat (grams)	0.6 g
Total Fat	4 g	Cholesterol (mg)	0 mg
% Fat	18	Sodium (mg)	560 mg

Above figures based on per serving basis.

HERBED TOMATO SOUP

¼ tsp. olive oil
2 Tbsp. chopped onion
2 Tbsp. chopped celery
½ c. chopped canned
   tomatoes
½ c. canned beef broth
⅛ tsp. crushed dried
   basil
⅛ tsp. oregano leaves
½ bay leaf
Freshly ground pepper
2 tsp. chopped fresh
   basil or parsley to
   garnish

In small nonstick saucepot, heat olive oil. Add chopped onion and celery; cook, stirring occasionally, for 5 minutes or until soft (could add 1 tsp. water to help "saute" vegetables). Stir in remaining ingredients, except fresh basil or parsley. Bring to a boil over medium heat. Reduce heat to low; cover and cook for 5 minutes. Remove and discard bay leaf. Pour the contents into blender and process until smooth. Pour back into saucepot and heat just to a boil. Pour into large mug or bowl and garnish soup with fresh basil or parsley. Serves 1.

NUTRITIONAL INFORMATION

Calories	55	Sat. Fat (grams)	0.4 g
Total Fat	2 g	Cholesterol (mg)	0 mg
% Fat	27	Sodium (mg)	601 mg

Above figures based on per serving basis.

MARYLAND OYSTER STEW

1 c. evaporated skimmed
   milk
36 shucked Eastern
   oysters and their liquor
½ c. diced celery,
   blanched
½ c. diced onion,
   blanched
½ tsp. freshly ground
   white pepper
½ tsp. sweet paprika
2 Tbsp. minced fresh
   parsley

In medium saucepan over medium heat, heat milk (do not boil). Add remaining ingredients, except parsley. Simmer for about 4 minutes or until oysters are opaque and edges curl. Stir in parsley. Serve at once. Serves 4.

NUTRITIONAL INFORMATION	
Calories 148	Sat. Fat (grams) .... 1.1 g
Total Fat .... 3 g	Cholesterol (mg) .... 69 mg
% Fat 21	Sodium (mg) .... 354 mg

Above figures based on per serving basis.

POTATO SOUP

8 pared, diced potatoes
4 pared, sliced carrots
4 stalks celery, diced
1 onion, chopped
1 can skim evaporated
   milk
2 qt. water
¼ tsp. marjoram
½ tsp. paprika
½ tsp. pepper
2 tsp. parsley flakes

Cook vegetables until tender. Stir in 1 can skim evaporated milk. Sprinkle with imitation bacon bits. Serve hot with crackers. Serves 12.

NUTRITIONAL INFORMATION	
Calories 100	Sat. Fat (grams) .... 0 g
Total Fat ...... less than 1 g	Cholesterol (mg) .... 1 mg
% Fat 2	Sodium (mg) .... 62 mg

Above figures based on per serving basis.

BROCCOLI SALAD

3 c. broccoli flowerets
   and coarsely chopped
   stems
⅔ c. raw peanuts
1 c. raisins
2 green onions, chopped
1 c. no-oil bottled salad
   dressing

Combine all ingredients and toss lightly. Serves 8.

NUTRITIONAL INFORMATION	
Calories 171	Sat. Fat (grams) .... 1 g
Total Fat .... 6 g	Cholesterol (mg) .... 0 mg
% Fat 30	Sodium (mg) .... 375 mg

Above figures based on per serving basis.

CARROT-APPLE SALAD

2 large Granny Smith
   apples
2 tsp. lemon juice
5 carrots, shredded
2 stalks celery, diced
½ c. raisins
¼ c. walnuts, chopped
½ c. plain lowfat yogurt
¼ c. orange juice

Core unpeeled apples and cut into chunks. Sprinkle them with lemon juice. Add remaining lemon juice, carrots, celery, raisins, and walnuts in small bowl. Combine yogurt and orange juice dressing; blend dressing with the fruit mixture. Refrigerate overnight. Serves 10.

NUTRITIONAL INFORMATION	
Calories...............87	Sat. Fat (grams).......0.3 g
Total Fat...............2 g	Cholesterol (mg).........1 mg
% Fat....................21	Sodium (mg)............30 mg

Above figures based on per serving basis.

CHICKEN SALAD SUPREME

2 pkg. lime jello
3 c. hot water
¼ c. lemon juice
1 c. fat free mayonnaise
2 c. chopped chicken
1 (No. 2) can pineapple
   chunks, drained
½ c. toasted almonds

Dissolve jello in hot water. Add lemon juice and mayonnaise. Cool until mixture begins to thicken, then beat until light and fluffy. Fold in chicken, pineapple, and almonds. Pour into 1 quart mold and chill. Serves 6 to 8.

NUTRITIONAL INFORMATION	
Calories...............304	Sat. Fat (grams).......1.5 g
Total Fat...............10 g	Cholesterol (mg).......36 mg
% Fat....................29	Sodium (mg)..........338 mg

Above figures based on per serving basis.

COMPANY COLESLAW

1 small (1¾ lb.) head
   cabbage, coarsely
   chopped
1 (20 oz.) can
   unsweetened crushed
   pineapple
1½ c. grated carrot
1 c. chopped celery
¼ c. raisins
¼ c. lowfat mayonnaise

Combine all ingredients in a large bowl; toss. Cover and refrigerate overnight. Serves 11.

NUTRITIONAL INFORMATION	
Calories...............84	Sat. Fat (grams)..........0 g
Total Fat...............1 g	Cholesterol (mg).........1 mg
% Fat....................14	Sodium (mg)............59 mg

Above figures based on per serving basis.

CRANBERRY SALAD

1 (9 oz.) can crushed
  pineapple, drained
3 (3 oz.) pkg. cherry
  gelatin
2 c. hot water
½ c. cold water
½ c. pineapple syrup
2 Tbsp. lemon juice
Dash of salt
¾ c. sugar or equivalent
  sugar substitute
1 (16 oz.) pkg. ground
  cranberries
½ c. finely ground
  orange with peel
1 c. orange sections
¾ c. chopped celery
⅓ c. coarsely chopped
  walnuts

Drain pineapple; reserve syrup. Dissolve gelatin in boiling water. Add cold water, pineapple syrup, lemon juice, and salt. Chill. Add sugar to fruits and let stand until gelatin firms. Combine fruit mixture with gelatin and pour into mold, rinsed first with cold water. Refrigerate until serving time. Serves 10 to 12.

NUTRITIONAL INFORMATION			
Calories	231	Sat. Fat (grams)	0 g
Total Fat	2 g	Cholesterol (mg)	0 mg
% Fat	9	Sodium (mg)	67 mg

Above figures based on per serving basis.

CUCUMBER AND CITRUS SALAD

2 cucumbers, peeled and
  cut into 2 inch
  segments
1 tsp. chopped fresh
  rosemary or ¼ tsp.
  crushed dried rosemary
1 tsp. olive oil
Freshly ground black
  pepper to taste
2 pink grapefruits
3 navel oranges
2 Tbsp. fresh lime juice
¼ c. fresh orange juice
¼ c. fresh grapefruit
  juice
1 tsp. red wine vinegar
¼ tsp. salt
1 scallion, sliced thin

Remove the core of seeds from each cucumber segment, using a melon baller or a small spoon. Slice the segments into ⅛ inch thick rings. Toss the rings with the rosemary, oil, and pepper; set aside. Cut away the peel, white pith and outer membrane from the grapefruit and oranges. Separate the segments from the inner membrane by slicing to the core on either side of each segment. Set them aside.

Arrange the cucumber slices and citrus slices on a deep platter. Combine the lime juice, orange juice, grapefruit juice, vinegar, and salt. Pour this dressing over the salad. Sprinkle the scallion slices over the top. Serves 4.

NUTRITIONAL INFORMATION			
Calories	131	Sat. Fat (grams)	0 g
Total Fat	2 g	Cholesterol (mg)	0 mg
% Fat	10	Sodium (mg)	138 mg

Above figures based on per serving basis.

FRUIT SALAD WITH CITRUS DRESSING

1 large Red Delicious
apple, cored and diced
1 medium banana,
diagonally sliced
1/4 c. plus 1 Tbsp. lemon
juice, divided
1 1/2 c. sliced fresh
strawberries
1/4 c. unsweetened
orange juice
1 1/2 tsp. cornstarch
2 Tbsp. sugar
6 curly leaf lettuce leaves

Combine apple and banana in a medium bowl. Sprinkle with 1 tablespoon lemon juice. Add strawberry slices; toss gently and set aside. Combine orange juice, remaining 1/4 cup lemon juice, and cornstarch in a small saucepan; stir until smooth. Add sugar, stirring well to combine. Bring mixture to a boil. Reduce heat to medium; cook, stirring constantly, until thickened and bubbly. Remove from heat and let cool. Pour orange juice mixture over reserved fruit mixture. Toss gently to coat well.

Place lettuce leaves on 6 individual salad plates. Spoon 1/2 cup fruit mixture onto each lettuce leaf. Serve immediately. Serves 6.

NUTRITIONAL INFORMATION			
Calories	74	Sat. Fat (grams)	0 g
Total Fat	less than 1 g	Cholesterol (mg)	0 mg
% Fat	3	Sodium (mg)	3 mg

Above figures based on per serving basis.

FRUITED CHICKEN SALAD

2 c. (8 oz.) skinless
diced, cooked chicken
breast
1 c. diced celery
1 c. seedless grapes,
halved
1/2 c. canned
unsweetened crushed
pineapple, drained
2 Tbsp. slivered almonds
1/2 tsp. salt
1/4 c. light sour cream
1 Tbsp. low cal
mayonnaise

Combine all ingredients and chill. Serve on lettuce cups. Makes 4 (1 cup) servings.

NUTRITIONAL INFORMATION			
Calories	199	Sat. Fat (grams)	2.0 g
Total Fat	7 g	Cholesterol (mg)	54 mg
% Fat	29	Sodium (mg)	365 mg

Above figures based on per serving basis.

FRUIT SALAD WITH DRESSING

4 bananas, sliced
1 (15½ oz.) can
  pineapple tidbits,
  drained
½ c. red seedless grapes,
  halved
½ c. white seedless
  grapes, halved
2 (11 oz.) cans mandarin
  oranges, drained
3 apples, diced

Dressing:
½ c. sugar
Grated rind from 1
  orange
¼ c. lemon juice
¼ c. orange juice
¾ c. pineapple juice
2 Tbsp. cornstarch
¼ c. cold water

Mix sugar, rind, and juices in a saucepan. Bring to a boil. Add cornstarch that has been dissolved in cold water. Stir constantly over medium heat till thick. Cool.

Mix fruit in large bowl. Pour dressing over and stir well. Serves 10-12.

NUTRITIONAL INFORMATION		
Calories.................170	Sat. Fat (grams)..........0 g	
Total Fat....................1 g	Cholesterol (mg).........0 mg	
% Fat.......................3	Sodium (mg)..............4 mg	

Above figures based on per serving basis.

OLD-FASHIONED FRUIT SALAD

1 (15 oz.) can pineapple
  chunks
½ c. sugar
3 apples (unpeeled),
  chopped
3 oranges, peeled,
  seeded and sectioned
3 bananas, sliced
1 c. miniature
  marshmallows
1 c. chopped pecans or
  walnuts
1 c. grapes, cut in halves

Drain pineapple, reserving ¼ cup juice. Combine reserved juice and sugar; stir well and set aside. Combine remaining ingredients. Pour pineapple juice mixture over salad and toss gently. Chill for 1 hour. Serves 12.

NUTRITIONAL INFORMATION		
Calories.................203	Sat. Fat (grams).......0.6 g	
Total Fat....................7 g	Cholesterol (mg).........0 mg	
% Fat.......................29	Sodium (mg)..............3 mg	

Above figures based on per serving basis.

OLD-FASHIONED POTATO SALAD

**4 medium size potatoes
(about 1 lb.)
½ c. finely chopped
celery
½ c. finely chopped
green bell pepper
¼ c. chopped onion
¼ c. chopped dill pickle
(or sweet)
¼ c. chopped fresh
parsley
1 Tbsp. chopped
pimento
2 hard-boiled eggs
(discard yolks -
optional)**

**Dressing:
¾ c. nonfat yogurt
1 Tbsp. Dijon mustard
1 Tbsp. lemon juice
1 tsp. grated lemon rind
¼ tsp. ground black
pepper**

Peel potatoes and cut into quarters. Cook in boiling water until tender, about 15 to 20 minutes. Drain and cool to room temperature. Place potatoes in a large bowl and mix with celery, pepper, onion, pickle, parsley, pimento, and egg. Beat together dressing ingredients; pour over salad and toss. Serve chilled. Serves 4.

NUTRITIONAL INFORMATION	
Calories.................161	Sat. Fat (grams).......1.0 g
Total Fat....................3 g	Cholesterol (mg).....107 mg
% Fat.....................18	Sodium (mg)..........306 mg

Above figures based on per serving basis.

ORANGE AMBROSIA SALAD

**2 fresh oranges, peeled
and cut into chunks
1 banana, sliced
8 oz. pineapple chunks
(canned or fresh)
½ c. miniature
marshmallows**

**Dressing:
¾ c. lowfat cottage
cheese
2 Tbsp. skim milk
2 tsp. lemon juice**

In a medium bowl, combine fruit and marshmallows.

For dressing: Mix all ingredients in a blender on medium speed until smooth and creamy. Pour dressing over fruit and lightly toss. Chill and serve. Serves 6.

NUTRITIONAL INFORMATION	
Calories.................96	Sat. Fat (grams).......0.4 g
Total Fat....................1 g	Cholesterol (mg).........2 mg
% Fat.....................8	Sodium (mg)..........120 mg

Above figures based on per serving basis.

ORANGE DELIGHT

1 large pkg. orange jello
2 c. boiling water
4 c. ice cubes
2 (8 oz.) plain lowfat
  yogurt
2 c. mandarin orange
  slices (no sugar)
1 tsp. vanilla extract

Dissolve jello in water. Add ice cubes. Stir until thickened, 3 to 5 minutes. Remove unmelted ice. Gently stir in drained orange slices and vanilla. Fold in yogurt. Refrigerate until firm. (Other fruits also good - strawberries or raspberries.) Makes 12 (½ cup) servings.

NUTRITIONAL INFORMATION	
Calories..................80	Sat. Fat (grams).......0.4 g
Total Fat..................1 g	Cholesterol (mg).........2 mg
% Fat......................7	Sodium (mg) ....64 mg

Above figures based on per serving basis.

RASPBERRY DELIGHT

2 env. raspberry diet
  gelatin
2 c. boiling water
1 (20 oz.) pkg. frozen
  raspberries (no sugar
  added)
2 c. unsweetened
  applesauce

Dissolve gelatin in boiling water. Add berries; stir till berries have thawed. Stir in applesauce. Pour into serving bowl and chill until set. Makes 12 (½ cup) servings.

May be topped with low calorie topping.

NUTRITIONAL INFORMATION	
Calories..................46	Sat. Fat (grams)..........0 g
Total Fat......less than 1 g	Cholesterol (mg).........0 mg
% Fat......................5	Sodium (mg) ....37 mg

Above figures based on per serving basis.

STUFFED CHERRY TOMATOES

16 cherry tomatoes (½
  pt. container)
1 (3¼ oz.) can low
  sodium tuna in water,
  drained and flaked (¾
  c.)
2 Tbsp. plain lowfat
  yogurt
2 tsp. finely chopped
  green onion
2 tsp. low sodium chili
  sauce
¼ tsp. prepared
  horseradish
⅛ tsp. ground black
  pepper

With a sharp knife, slice tops of tomatoes. With a grapefruit spoon, remove pulp; drain upside down on paper towels.

In small bowl, combine remaining ingredients. Spoon an equal amount into each tomato. Refrigerate for about 1 hour. Serves 4.

NUTRITIONAL INFORMATION	
Calories..................46	Sat. Fat (grams)..........0 g
Total Fat......less than 1 g	Cholesterol (mg).........4 mg
% Fat......................8	Sodium (mg) ....21 mg

Above figures based on per serving basis.

TACO SALAD

2 (15½ oz.) cans kidney
   beans, drained and
   rinsed
1 (15 oz.) can tomato
   puree
2 tsp. onion flakes
2 tsp. chili powder
1 head iceberg or other
   lettuce, chopped
1 bunch green onions,
   chopped
2 ripe tomatoes,
   chopped
1 large green pepper,
   chopped
4 oz. low sodium, skim
   milk Cheddar cheese,
   shredded
1 (8 oz.) pkg. low sodium
   nacho chips

Cook tomato puree over medium heat until thickened. Add onion flakes, chili powder, and beans; set aside.

Chop lettuce, onions, tomatoes, and green pepper for salad. Arrange crunched nacho chips on bottom of large flat platter. Top with salad. Spread cooled tomato sauce over salad and finish with shredded cheese. Serves 6.

NUTRITIONAL INFORMATION

Calories	384	Sat. Fat (grams)	2.8 g
Total Fat	12 g	Cholesterol (mg)	4 mg
% Fat	27	Sodium (mg)	323 mg

Above figures based on per serving basis.

TANGY CITRUS SALAD

3 c. cubed fresh
   pineapple
3 c. grapefruit sections
1 tsp. vanilla extract
1 (8 oz.) ctn. lemon
   lowfat yogurt
12 Boston lettuce leaves

Combine pineapple and grapefruit; cover and chill. Stir vanilla into yogurt. Line 6 individual plates with 2 lettuce leaves each; place 1 cup fruit on lettuce. Spoon 2 tablespoons yogurt mixture over each serving. Serves 6.

NUTRITIONAL INFORMATION

Calories	111	Sat. Fat (grams)	0.3 g
Total Fat	1 g	Cholesterol (mg)	2 mg
% Fat	7	Sodium (mg)	26 mg

Above figures based on per serving basis.

TURKEY SALAD

2 c. skinless cooked
   white meat turkey,
   diced
½ c. minced onion
½ c. chopped celery with
   leaves
¼ c. minced fresh
   parsley
5 Tbsp. fat free
   mayonnaise
2 Tbsp. light sour cream
   or yogurt
1 Tbsp. safflower oil
1 tsp. apple cider vinegar

Mix last 7 ingredients together. Add meat and mix well. Chill well and serve. Serves 4.

For *Herbed Turkey* or *Chicken Salad*, add 1 tablespoon of your favorite fresh herbs or 1 teaspoon dried.

NUTRITIONAL INFORMATION

Calories	162	Sat. Fat (grams)	1.1 g
Total Fat	5 g	Cholesterol (mg)	63 mg
% Fat	29	Sodium (mg)	191 mg

Above figures based on per serving basis.

GERMAN SWEET-SOUR GREEN BEANS

1 oz. Canadian bacon,
   diced
⅓ c. diced onions
1 (16 oz.) can French cut
   green beans
2 Tbsp. salad vinegar
1 Tbsp. flour
2 tsp. sugar

Spray nonstick saucepan with low calorie cooking spray. Fry bacon in pan until crisp. Add onions and cook until tender. Drain green beans, reserving ⅓ cup liquid. Combine liquid with vinegar, flour, and sugar. Stir into saucepan. Cook and stir until thickened. Add beans and heat through. Serves 4.

NUTRITIONAL INFORMATION

Calories	45	Sat. Fat (grams)	0 g
Total Fat	1 g	Cholesterol (mg)	4 mg
% Fat	13	Sodium (mg)	362 mg

Above figures based on per serving basis.

CREAMY CORN CASSEROLE

1 Tbsp. melted
   margarine
1 tsp. flour
1 tsp. powdered chicken
   bouillon
1 tsp. seasoned salt
¼ tsp. dry mustard
2 tsp. dried chopped
   chives
1 tsp. parsley flakes
2 c. whole kernel corn,
   drained
1 c. whipped lowfat
   cottage cheese

Preheat oven to 325°. Whip cottage cheese in blender for 2 minutes. Blend the margarine with the flour until smooth. Add seasonings, drained canned or cooked frozen corn, and cottage cheese. Mix well and pour into a 1½ quart casserole. Bake for 25 to 30 minutes or until heated through. Garnish with green pepper rings and pimiento curls if desired. Serves 6.

NUTRITIONAL INFORMATION	
Calories.................101	Sat. Fat (grams).......0.9 g
Total Fat...................3 g	Cholesterol (mg).........3 mg
% Fat.....................28	Sodium (mg) ....755 mg

Above figures based on per serving basis.

CUCUMBERS IN SOUR CREAM-YOGURT

2 cucumbers, sliced
   (enough to equal 2 c.)
2 Tbsp. apple cider
   vinegar
2 tsp. safflower oil
½ c. fat free plain yogurt
   and ½ c. fat free sour
   cream
½ c. chopped onion
1 tsp. dill weed or seed

Mix last 5 ingredients together. Add cucumbers. Mix well. Refrigerate. Serves 4.

NUTRITIONAL INFORMATION	
Calories...................84	Sat. Fat (grams).......0.3 g
Total Fat...................2 g	Cholesterol (mg).........1 mg
% Fat.....................26	Sodium (mg) ....48 mg

Above figures based on per serving basis.

LEMON PECAN WILD RICE

2 c. water
2 c. canned chicken
    broth
Rind of ½ lemon,
    removed with a
    vegetable peeler and
    cut into julienne strips
1½ Tbsp. fresh lemon
    juice
2 tsp. unsalted margarine
1 c. wild rice, rinsed and
    drained
⅓ c. pecans, toasted and
    chopped
1 c. brown rice
¼ c. minced fresh
    parsley leaves
3 Tbsp. chopped scallion

In a saucepan, combine the broth, water, lemon juice, margarine, and half the lemon rind. Bring to a boil and stir in the wild rice and brown rice. Cook the rice, covered, over low heat for 50 minutes to 1 hour, until rice is tender and water is absorbed. Stir in pecans, scallions, parsley, remaining lemon rind, and salt and pepper to taste. Serves 8.

NUTRITIONAL INFORMATION	
Calories................159	Sat. Fat (grams).......0.7 g
Total Fat...................5 g	Cholesterol (mg).........0 mg
% Fat.....................30	Sodium (mg)..........198 mg

Above figures based on per serving basis.

MARINATED CUCUMBERS

6 medium cucumbers
1 medium onion
Salt
Pepper
2½ tsp. olive oil
1 Tbsp. white vinegar
Garlic powder (optional)

Slice cucumbers very thin into bowl. Chop onion and add to bowl. Add salt, pepper, olive oil, and vinegar (garlic powder if desired). Marinate for at least 2 hours in refrigerator before serving. Use as a side dish or add to any green salad. Serves 6.

NUTRITIONAL INFORMATION	
Calories...................64	Sat. Fat (grams).......0.4 g
Total Fat...................2 g	Cholesterol (mg).........0 mg
% Fat.....................29	Sodium (mg)...........95 mg

Above figures based on per serving basis.

MARINATED VEGETABLES

1 (1 lb.) pkg. carrots
1 bunch broccoli
1 head cauliflower
1 lb. fresh mushrooms
¼ c. corn oil
3 c. tarragon vinegar
½ c. sugar
1 tsp. garlic powder
1 Tbsp. Dijon mustard
2 tsp. salt
1½ tsp. large grain
  pepper
1 pt. cherry tomatoes
1 c. fresh sliced squash

Wash and cut vegetables into bite-size pieces. Place in large glass bowl. Pour marinade over vegetables and chill for several hours before serving. Serves 12.

NUTRITIONAL INFORMATION	
Calories...............140	Sat. Fat (grams).......0.7 g
Total Fat................5.3 g	Cholesterol (mg).........0 mg
% Fat.....................28	Sodium (mg)..........438 mg

Above figures based on per serving basis.

MEXI SCRAMBLE

Nonstick spray
1 medium green pepper,
  chopped
1 medium onion,
  chopped
1 medium tomato,
  chopped
½ c. frozen whole kernel
  corn
1 (15 oz.) can pinto
  beans, drained and
  coarsely chopped
4 egg whites, beaten
½ c. shredded sharp
  Cheddar cheese (Swiss
  or Mozzarella)
¼ c. salsa sauce
Salt and pepper to taste
  (optional)

Spray nonstick skillet with nonstick spray. Heat over medium heat; saute green pepper and onion until tender. Stir in tomato, corn, and beans. Add egg whites and cheese; stir as for scrambled eggs. Season with salt and pepper if desired. Serve with salsa. Serves 4 to 6.

NUTRITIONAL INFORMATION	
Calories...............142	Sat. Fat (grams).......2.4 g
Total Fat................4 g	Cholesterol (mg).......12 mg
% Fat.....................27	Sodium (mg)..........355 mg

Above figures based on per serving basis.

ORANGE-SPICED CARROTS

3 c. sliced carrots
¼ c. water
¼ c. unsweetened
 orange juice
1 tsp. grated orange rind
1 Tbsp. reduced-calorie
 margarine
¼ tsp. ground nutmeg
½ tsp. vanilla extract
2 tsp. chopped fresh
 parsley

Combine first 3 ingredients in a small saucepan. Cover and simmer for 5 to 7 minutes or until carrots are crisp-tender. Add orange rind and next 3 ingredients; stir well. Garnish with parsley. Serves 5.

NUTRITIONAL INFORMATION	
Calories...................60	Sat. Fat (grams).......0.3 g
Total Fat...................2 g	Cholesterol (mg).........0 mg
% Fat......................24	Sodium (mg)............46 mg

Above figures based on per serving basis.

ORIENTAL VEGETABLE STIR-FRY

1 tsp. peanut or
 safflower oil
½ c. diagonally sliced
 green onions
½ garlic clove, minced
1 c. diagonally sliced
 celery (thin)
¾ c. snow peas
½ c. diced red bell
 pepper
⅓ c. water
2 tsp. soy sauce
1 tsp. cornstarch
⅛ tsp. ground ginger
Dash of salt and pepper

Heat oil over high heat in skillet or wok. Add onions and garlic; stir-fry for 1 minute. Add celery, peas, and pepper; stir quickly and often for 2 minutes.

Combine water, soy sauce, and cornstarch in small bowl; stir to dissolve and pour over mixture. Add ginger, salt, and pepper; cook, stirring constantly, until sauce is thickened. Serves 2.

NUTRITIONAL INFORMATION	
Calories...................77	Sat. Fat (grams).......0.4 g
Total Fat...................3 g	Cholesterol (mg).........0 mg
% Fat......................28	Sodium (mg)..........564 mg

Above figures based on per serving basis.

HERBED NEW POTATOES

4 small new potatoes
1 Tbsp. melted diet
 margarine
1½ tsp. dried dill weed
 (or to taste)

Slice new potatoes. Steam until tender on stove or in microwave. Season with melted margarine and dill weed. Serves 4.

NUTRITIONAL INFORMATION	
Calories...................90	Sat. Fat (grams).......0.3 g
Total Fat...................2 g	Cholesterol (mg).........0 mg
% Fat......................20	Sodium (mg)............22 mg

Above figures based on per serving basis.

POTATO PANCAKES

**6 medium potatoes,
    peeled and coarsely
    grated
1 large onion, coarsely
    grated
¼ c. milk
1 carrot, finely grated
1 egg white and 1 whole
    egg, lightly beaten, or
    1 container pasteurized
    egg substitute
½ c. flour
1 tsp. salt (optional)
Black pepper to taste
Oil (for frying)**

Place grated potatoes and onion in a colander over a large bowl and press the vegetables to squeeze out excess liquid. Let stand for 5 minutes and press again. Pour off liquid, but save any starch collected at the bottom. Add potato mixture to the bowl along with carrot, eggs, flour, salt, and pepper. Stir the ingredients to combine.

In a large nonstick pan, heat a small amount of oil till very hot. Place about ¼ cup of butter for each pancake and fry a few at a time. Turn when golden brown on the bottom. Turn only once. Set on paper towels laid over a rack and keep warm in a preheated low oven until ready, with applesauce or lowfat yogurt. Serves 12.

NUTRITIONAL INFORMATION		
Calories..................93	Sat. Fat (grams)..........0 g	
Total Fat...................1 g	Cholesterol (mg).......18 mg	
% Fat.......................7	Sodium (mg)..........197 mg	

Above figures based on per serving basis.

SCALLOPED POTATOES

**2 Tbsp. liquid margarine
1 Tbsp. flour
1½ c. skim milk
4 potatoes, peeled and
    sliced
1 onion, sliced
Salt and pepper**

Melt margarine; stir in flour. Add milk slowly, stirring constantly. Cook and stir over low heat till thickened. Season to taste with salt and pepper. Place potatoes and onions in baking dish; pour in sauce. Bake for about 45 minutes at 350°. Serves 6.

Variations: Sprinkle with bacon bits (imitation) or Mozzarella cheese before baking.

NUTRITIONAL INFORMATION		
Calories..................126	Sat. Fat (grams).......0.7 g	
Total Fat...................4 g	Cholesterol (mg).........1 mg	
% Fat.......................28	Sodium (mg)..........73 mg	

Above figures based on per serving basis.

STUFFED BAKED POTATOES

4 large (about 7 oz.)
 baked potatoes
½ c. lowfat or skim milk,
 warmed
1 c. part-skim Ricotta
2 small cloves garlic,
 crushed
¼ tsp. salt (if desired)
⅛ tsp. freshly ground
 black pepper
2 c. chopped, cooked
 broccoli (stems or
 flowerets) or spinach
¼ c. grated Parmesan,
 divided

Take thin slices off the potatoes lengthwise. With a melon baller or small sharp spoon, carefully scoop out the flesh, without tearing the skin. Reserve the skins (but not the slices).

In a medium bowl, mash the potato flesh with the warm milk. Combine it well with the Ricotta, garlic, salt, pepper, broccoli or spinach, and 2 tablespoons Parmesan. Stuff the potato mixture into the reserved potato skins, piling it high. Sprinkle the stuffed potatoes with the remaining cheese. Place the potatoes in a pan and bake them in a preheated 350° oven for 20 minutes (longer if the potatoes were cold to start with). Serves 4.

NUTRITIONAL INFORMATION	
Calories.................353	Sat. Fat (grams).......4.7 g
Total Fat...................8 g	Cholesterol (mg).......26 mg
% Fat.....................19	Sodium (mg)..........377 mg

Above figures based on per serving basis.

TWICE BAKED POTATOES

4 medium potatoes,
 baked
1 c. lowfat cottage
 cheese
½ c. lowfat milk
1 Tbsp. onion, minced
Freshly ground black
 pepper
Paprika
Dried parsley flakes

Cut hot potatoes in halves lengthwise. Scoop out potatoes, leaving skins intact for restuffing.

With wire whisk, beat potatoes with cottage cheese, milk, and onion. Spoon mixture back into skins. Sprinkle with paprika, parsley flakes, and black pepper. Bake for 10 minutes or until just golden. Serves 8.

NUTRITIONAL INFORMATION	
Calories.................100	Sat. Fat (grams).......0.5 g
Total Fat...................1 g	Cholesterol (mg).........4 mg
% Fat.....................8	Sodium (mg)..........127 mg

Above figures based on per serving basis.

MAIN DISHES

BBQ MEATBALLS

½ lb. ground sirloin
½ lb. skinless white meat
  turkey, ground
½ c. bread crumbs
½ tsp. garlic salt
¼ tsp. pepper
⅛ c. catsup

Sauce:
½ bottle barbeque sauce
1 small can tomato sauce
2 Tbsp. flour
½ c. water

Mix all of the ingredients and roll into small balls. Place in baking dish and cook for 30 minutes at 250°. Drain off any grease.

Pour sauce over the meatballs and cook for 20 more minutes. Garnish with stuffed olives if desired. Makes 7 servings of 3 meatballs each.

NUTRITIONAL INFORMATION	
Calories..................164	Sat. Fat (grams).......1.1 g
Total Fat...................3 g	Cholesterol (mg).......44 mg
% Fat.....................19	Sodium (mg)..........730 mg

Above figures based on per serving basis.

BEEF PIZZA

Tomato-Basil Sauce:
1 (28 oz.) can chopped
  tomatoes
1 Tbsp. dried basil
½ tsp. salt
¼ tsp. freshly ground
  black pepper

Topping:
1½ lb. top round, fat
  trimmed, ground
3 Japanese eggplants (or
  zucchini), thinly sliced
  (1 lb.)
6 cloves garlic, finely
  chopped
¼ c. freshly grated
  Parmesan cheese

8 tortillas

Tomato-Basil Sauce: Mix all ingredients in a bowl.

Chop vegetables and grate cheese. Heat oven to 450°. Place tortillas on baking sheets and bake for 5 minutes. Remove from oven. Brown beef in nonstick skillet. Drain off excess fat as it accumulates. Top each tortilla with about ⅓ cup Tomato-Basil Sauce and about ⅛ of each of the toppings. Bake for 10 minutes longer or until tortilla is lightly browned and topping is bubbly. Serves 8.

NUTRITIONAL INFORMATION	
Calories..................282	Sat. Fat (grams).......2.1 g
Total Fat...................7 g	Cholesterol (mg).......55 mg
% Fat.....................22	Sodium (mg)..........563 mg

Above figures based on per serving basis.

CHILI

2 lb. cubed stewing beef
1 c. chopped onions
1 green pepper, chopped
1 clove garlic
1½ Tbsp. chili powder
2 jalapeno peppers
½ tsp. cumin
½ tsp. oregano
½ tsp. salt
2½ c. water
1 (15 oz.) can pinto
   beans, drained
Cooking spray

Spray large non-stick pan with cooking spray; brown beef well. Add onions, green pepper, and garlic; cook with beef for 10 minutes. Add all the remaining ingredients, except beans. Simmer chili for 1½ hours. Add beans and simmer for 30 minutes longer. Serves 8.

NUTRITIONAL INFORMATION		
Calories.................213	Sat. Fat (grams).......2.4 g	
Total Fat...................7 g	Cholesterol (mg).......78 mg	
% Fat......................30	Sodium (mg)..........268 mg	

Above figures based on per serving basis.

BEEF STROGANOFF

2 small sirloin strips
2 tsp. corn oil
1 onion, finely chopped
1 can mushrooms
1 clove minced garlic
1 beef bouillon cube
1 (8 oz.) ctn. fat free
   sour cream
1 c. hot water
8 oz. noodles

Cut sirloin in small strips. Brown in oil till medium rare and remove from pan. Saute onions and garlic in remaining oil. Add mushrooms and bouillon cube that has been dissolved in hot water. Simmer for 5 minutes. Add meat and sour cream. Heat thoroughly. Serve on noodles. Serves 4.

NUTRITIONAL INFORMATION		
Calories.................353	Sat. Fat (grams).......3.6 g	
Total Fat.................11 g	Cholesterol (mg).......87 mg	
% Fat......................30	Sodium (mg)..........481 mg	

Above figures based on per serving basis.

COUNTRY-FRIED STEAK

**4 (4 oz.) slices lean,
 cubed sirloin steak
½ tsp. lemon pepper
 seasoning
Vegetable cooking spray
4 (¼ inch) slices onion
1 tsp. beef flavored
 bouillon granules (no
 salt added if desired)
1 c. hot water
1 Tbsp. cornstarch
¼ c. water
2 c. cooked rice**

Sprinkle steak with lemon pepper seasoning; set aside. Coat a nonstick skillet with cooking spray. Place over medium heat until hot. Add steak and cook until browned, turning once. Place an onion slice on top of each piece of steak.

Combine bouillon granules and hot water, stirring well. Add bouillon mixture to skillet. Bring to a boil. Reduce heat and simmer, uncovered, for 10 minutes. Remove steak to serving platter; keep warm.

Combine cornstarch and water; stir into bouillon mixture in skillet. Cook over medium heat, stirring constantly, until thickened and bubbly. Serve steak and gravy over rice.

Steak may be placed back into gravy and simmered a short time or until ready to serve. Serves 4.

NUTRITIONAL INFORMATION	
Calories.................343	Sat. Fat (grams).......3.0 g
Total Fat....................8 g	Cholesterol (mg).......82 mg
% Fat......................23	Sodium (mg)..........512 mg

Above figures based on per serving basis.

KOREAN BARBECUED BEEF

**1 lb. (1½ inches thick)
 top round steak
1 Tbsp. vegetable oil
¼ c. soy sauce
1 pkg. Sweet 'N Low or
 Equal
2 Tbsp. chopped green
 onion
1 Tbsp. sesame seed
¼ tsp. ginger
2 cloves garlic, minced**

Partially freeze beef. With sharp knife, cut very thin slices across grain. In small bowl, mix remaining ingredients. Place beef in heavy plastic bag in shallow dish. Pour in marinade and tie securely, turning several times, for at least 2 hours, preferably overnight. Drain beef. Reserve marinade. Broil beef on greased broiler pan 6 inches from source of heat for 10 to 12 minutes, basting frequently. Serves 4.

NUTRITIONAL INFORMATION	
Calories.................167	Sat. Fat (grams).......1.6 g
Total Fat....................5 g	Cholesterol (mg).......70 mg
% Fat......................30	Sodium (mg)..........381 mg

Above figures based on per serving basis.

MEATBALLS

1 lb. top round, fat
   trimmed, ground
¼ tsp. garlic salt
1 medium onion, finely
   chopped
¼ c. skim milk
½ tsp. salt
¼ tsp. pepper
¼ c. wheat germ
1 tsp. dry mustard
2 tsp. oil
1 (10½ oz.) can beef
   consomme
1 tsp. parsley flakes
   (dried or fresh)
1 Tbsp. cornstarch

Mix all ingredients, except the consomme. Form into 12 medium size meatballs. Heat the oil in a skillet and brown meatballs on all sides. Pour off any fat remaining in skillet and add the consomme. Sprinkle in the parsley flakes. Cover and cook gently for 20 minutes. Thicken the gravy with cornstarch. Makes 4 servings of 3 meatballs each.

NUTRITIONAL INFORMATION	
Calories.................231	Sat. Fat (grams).......1.9 g
Total Fat...................7 g	Cholesterol (mg).......71 mg
% Fat.....................29	Sodium (mg)..........606 mg

Above figures based on per serving basis.

POT ROAST OF BEEF

This particular roast is made with Italian seasonings.

2 lb. lean roast (top or
   bottom round,
   trimmed) or 2 lb. flank
   steak
4 cloves garlic, minced
2 medium onions, sliced
1 green pepper, sliced
4 stalks celery, cut in 2
   inch pieces
6 large carrots, cut in 2
   inch pieces
12 new potatoes
1 bay leaf
1 Tbsp. Italian
   seasonings
1 (28 oz.) can tomatoes
1 (15 oz.) can tomato
   sauce or puree
2 tsp. soy sauce
Dash of Worcestershire
Salt and pepper to taste

Place meat in a large roasting pan; cover with minced garlic, slices of onions, and green pepper. Place other vegetables and potatoes all around the meat.

Mix the soy sauce and Worcestershire sauce in either the tomatoes or the tomato sauce, then add both to the roast. Add all the other seasonings. Cook in a slow oven (250°) for 4 to 5 hours, or until meat falls apart when prodded with the tines of a fork. Serves 8.

NUTRITIONAL INFORMATION	
Calories.................304	Sat. Fat (grams).......2.1 g
Total Fat...................7 g	Cholesterol (mg).......70 mg
% Fat.....................20	Sodium (mg)..........671 mg

Above figures based on per serving basis.

SLIM SLOPPY JOES

1 lb. top round, fat
trimmed, ground
3 Tbsp. dehydrated
onion
½ c. mushrooms
½ green pepper,
chopped
Pinch of Sweet 'N Low
½ tsp. parsley
8 oz. tomato juice
Dash of Tabasco
Pinch of oregano

Brown meat in non-stick skillet and drain fat off. Return to skillet with remaining ingredients. Simmer until peppers are done, approximately 10 minutes. Serve over ½ hamburger roll. Serves 4 generously.

NUTRITIONAL INFORMATION	
Calories...............241	Sat. Fat (grams).......1.7 g
Total Fat................5 g	Cholesterol (mg).......70 mg
% Fat....................20	Sodium (mg)..........466 mg

Above figures based on per serving basis.

ORANGE-PINEAPPLE PORK CHOPS

4 (6 oz.) center cut pork
chops (½ inch thick)
Vegetable cooking spray
¼ tsp. salt
¼ tsp. pepper
1 c. unsweetened
pineapple juice,
divided
1 tsp. cornstarch
⅛ tsp. ground allspice
1 medium orange,
peeled, sectioned, and
seeded

Trim excess fat from chops and set aside. Coat a large skillet with cooking spray and place over medium high heat until hot. Add chops and brown on each side. Season with salt and pepper. Add ¾ cup pineapple juice and bring to a boil. Cover, reduce heat and cook for 45 minutes or until chops are tender.

Combine cornstarch, remaining ¼ cup pineapple juice, and allspice in small bowl; stir into skillet, cooking until thickened and bubbly, stirring constantly. Add orange sections and cook until thoroughly heated. Serves 4.

NUTRITIONAL INFORMATION	
Calories...............231	Sat. Fat (grams).......2.7 g
Total Fat................7 g	Cholesterol (mg).......75 mg
% Fat....................29	Sodium (mg)..........189 mg

Above figures based on per serving basis.

LUNCHTIME PORK IN PITA

⅓ c. (2 oz.) coarsely
  chopped, cooked,
  trimmed pork loin
1 Tbsp. light reduced-
  calorie mayonnaise
1 tsp. spicy brown
  mustard
¼ tsp. lemon juice
Dash of pepper
6 apple slices, cut ¼
  inch thick
¼ c. shredded lettuce
½ loaf pita bread

Combine mayonnaise, mustard, lemon juice, and pepper in small bowl. Add pork, tossing lightly to coat. Place apple slices, lettuce, and pork mixture in pita pocket. To carry to work, place sandwich in plastic bag or wrap; carry in an insulated bag. Serves 1.

NUTRITIONAL INFORMATION			
Calories	271	Sat. Fat (grams)	2.5 g
Total Fat	9 g	Cholesterol (mg)	49 mg
% Fat	30	Sodium (mg)	342 mg

Above figures based on per serving basis.

SAVORY PORK 'N POTATOES

4 pork loin rib chops (cut
  1 to 1¼ inches thick),
  trimmed
1 tsp. dried thyme leaves
½ tsp. ground sage
¼ tsp. ground allspice
1 tsp. oil
Salt
Pepper
¾ lb. sweet potatoes,
  pared and cut into ¼
  inch slices
2 c. water
2 Tbsp. honey
1 tsp. minced ginger root
2 small apples, cut into
  wedges

Combine thyme, sage, and allspice; rub on both sides of chops. Place chops on rack in broiler pan so surface of meat is 4 to 5 inches from heat. Broil at low to moderate temperature for 30 to 35 minutes, brushing with oil and turning occasionally. Season with salt and pepper.

Meanwhile, boil sweet potatoes, uncovered, in water, honey, ginger, and ¼ teaspoon salt for 5 minutes or until tender. Remove and reserve. Reduce cooking liquid to ¼ cup. Add apples and simmer for 3 minutes. Return potatoes to pan and heat through. Serve with pork chops. Serves 4.

NUTRITIONAL INFORMATION			
Calories	350	Sat. Fat (grams)	3.2 g
Total Fat	10 g	Cholesterol (mg)	68 mg
% Fat	25	Sodium (mg)	67 mg

Above figures based on per serving basis.

BAKED CHICKEN CACCIATORE

1 chicken, cut up and
  skinned in small pieces
2 c. crushed tomatoes
2 c. tomato puree
1 c. chopped onions
4 cloves garlic, minced
1 tsp. oregano
1 tsp. basil

Place chicken pieces in a lightly oiled baking pan. Bake for 30 minutes at 350°. Add onions and garlic. Bake for 15 more minutes. Add tomatoes and spices; turn chicken pieces to cover with tomato sauce and return to oven. Bake for an additional 30 minutes or until chicken is tender. Serves 4.

NUTRITIONAL INFORMATION			
Calories	309	Sat. Fat (grams)	1.3 g
Total Fat	5 g	Cholesterol (mg)	115 mg
% Fat	16	Sodium (mg)	817 mg

Above figures based on per serving basis.

BARBECUED CHICKEN BREASTS AND CAJUN RICE

4 chicken breasts,
  skinned (with the ribs)
1½ c. chicken stock
1 Tbsp. soy sauce
2 Tbsp. olive oil
½ tsp. garlic powder
½ tsp. pepper
Tabasco sauce to taste
½ tsp. paprika
1 tsp. basil
1 onion, chopped
2 green onions, chopped
1 green pepper, chopped
½ c. celery, chopped
1 c. white rice

Mix together all the ingredients, except the rice, and marinate for 2 to 3 hours. Warm the mixture in the microwave oven until warm to the touch. Remove the chicken and boil the marinade for 3 minutes, then add the rice. When it returns to a boil, cover and simmer for 20 to 30 minutes or until done.

Can check the rice halfway through the cooking to make sure that there is enough liquid; if not, add water. Ten minutes after the rice is started, brush the chicken with more olive oil and place on a hot grill. Turn the chicken every 5 minutes, brushing with olive oil at first, and add barbecue sauce (or even a little ketchup with some Tabasco sauce added) for the last turn. The chicken and the rice will be done at the same time. Serves 4.

NUTRITIONAL INFORMATION			
Calories	411	Sat. Fat (grams)	2.1 g
Total Fat	11 g	Cholesterol (mg)	73 mg
% Fat	24	Sodium (mg)	702 mg

Above figures based on per serving basis.

BREADED BREAST OF CHICKEN

2 whole chicken breasts,
skinned and split
1 c. fine dry bread
crumbs
1 Tbsp. chopped parsley
½ c. cholesterol free
pasteurized egg
substitute
2 Tbsp. corn oil
margarine
1 clove garlic, crushed
Lemon slices
Parsley

Pound chicken with mallet to flatten. Combine bread crumbs and parsley. Dip chicken into cholesterol free pasteurized egg substitute, then coat with bread crumb mixture and set aside.

In a large skillet, melt corn oil margarine over medium heat. Saute garlic until golden brown; discard clove. Place chicken in skillet and brown on both sides. Continue cooking until chicken is fork tender, about 3 to 4 minutes. Remove chicken from skillet onto platter. Garnish with lemon slices and sprigs of parsley. Serves 4.

NUTRITIONAL INFORMATION	
Calories.................270	Sat. Fat (grams).......1.7 g
Total Fat...................9 g	Cholesterol (mg).......69mg
% Fat.....................30	Sodium (mg).........315mg

Above figures based on per serving basis.

CHICKEN FAJITAS

2 Tbsp. fresh lime juice
1 Tbsp. minced onion
1 Tbsp. minced green
onion tops
1 clove garlic, minced
½ tsp. salt
½ tsp. pepper
½ tsp. cumin
1 lb. boneless, skinless
chicken breasts
4 (10½ inch) flour
tortillas, heated
2 c. shredded lettuce
1 tomato, diced
2 c. green, red or yellow
pepper
4 Tbsp. bottled salsa

Combine lime juice, onion, garlic, salt, pepper, and cumin in shallow dish. Add chicken, turning to coat. Cover and refrigerate for 4 hours or overnight.

Prepare grill or preheat broiler. Grill or broil chicken 4 inches from heat source for 4 minutes per side. Slice in strips ½ inch across the grain. Place chicken on heated tortillas and top with lettuce, tomato, pepper, and salsa. Serves 4.

NUTRITIONAL INFORMATION	
Calories.................344	Sat. Fat (grams).......1.0 g
Total Fat...................6 g	Cholesterol (mg).......66mg
% Fat.....................15	Sodium (mg).........779mg

Above figures based on per serving basis.

CHICKEN VEGETABLE DUMPLINGS

Stew:
1 broiler-fryer, cut up
2 c. sliced celery
2 c. sliced carrots
1 large onion, chopped
1 bay leaf
½ tsp. crumbled
   rosemary
1 (10 oz.) pkg. frozen
   green peas
1 qt. water, divided
Dumplings:
1 c. whole wheat pastry
   flour
1 c. oat flour
3 tsp. baking powder
½ tsp. sea salt
2 Tbsp. minced parsley
1 Tbsp. minced pimento
4 Tbsp. butter
¾ to 1 c. lowfat or skim
   milk

Stew: Remove skin from chicken. In a large pot, add meat, carrots, celery, onion, and herbs. Add water, half at a time, until barely covered. Use more if necessary. Bring to a boil; reduce heat and simmer for 15 minutes.

Dumplings: Meanwhile, prepare the dumpling mixture. Combine dry ingredients. Cut in butter. Add parsley, pimento, and enough milk to hold mixture together. Add peas to pot. When simmering, drop dumpling mixture by the tablespoonful into the hot broth. Cover and simmer for 20 minutes. Don't peek. Serve piping hot. Makes 5 servings.

NUTRITIONAL INFORMATION			
Calories	504	Sat. Fat (grams)	7.1 g
Total Fat	15 g	Cholesterol (mg)	118 mg
% Fat	26	Sodium (mg)	854 mg

Above figures based on per serving basis.

CRUNCHY OVEN-FRIED CHICKEN

1 c. crushed corn flakes
2 Tbsp. chopped fresh
   parsley
½ tsp. poultry seasoning
¼ tsp. lemon pepper
   seasoning
4 (6 oz.) chicken breast
   halves, skinned
¼ c. plain lowfat yogurt
Vegetable cooking spray

Combine cereal, chopped parsley, seasoning, and lemon pepper in a shallow dish. Brush chicken with yogurt and roll in cereal mixture. Place chicken on broiler pan, coated with cooking spray. Bake, uncovered, at 400° for 45 minutes or until done. Serves 4.

NUTRITIONAL INFORMATION			
Calories	298	Sat. Fat (grams)	0.7 g
Total Fat	2 g	Cholesterol (mg)	100 mg
% Fat	7	Sodium (mg)	412 mg

Above figures based on per serving basis.

HERBED CHICKEN STRIPS

1¼ c. uncooked oatmeal
1¼ tsp. basil
1 tsp. paprika
½ tsp. oregano
½ tsp. thyme
¼ tsp. garlic powder
2 whole chicken breasts,
  boned, skinned, and
  split
¼ c. skim milk
2 Tbsp. margarine,
  melted
1 (8 oz.) can tomato
  sauce
½ c. sliced green onion

Heat oven to 425°. Place oats in blender or food processor; cover. Blend for about 1 minute, stopping occasionally to stir. Cut chicken breasts in 1 inch strips. Coat chicken pieces in combined oat flour, 1 teaspoon basil, paprika, oregano, thyme, and garlic powder; dip into milk. Coat again with dry ingredients. Place in 15x10 inch jelly roll pan; brush with margarine. Bake for 25 to 30 minutes or until tender.

Combine tomato sauce, green onion, and remaining ¼ teaspoon basil; heat through, stirring occasionally. Serve with chicken. Serves 4.

NUTRITIONAL INFORMATION

Calories	309	Sat. Fat (grams)	1.7 g
Total Fat	9 g	Cholesterol (mg)	69 mg
% Fat	26	Sodium (mg)	498 mg

Above figures based on per serving basis.

ITALIAN CHICKEN CUTLETS

6 chicken breasts,
  halved, skinned, and
  boned
1 c. Italian seasoned
  bread crumbs
¼ c. Parmesan cheese
¼ c. all-purpose flour
2 Tbsp. wheat germ
  (optional)
1 (0.8 oz.) pkg. light
  Italian salad dressing
  mix
2 tsp. dried oregano
¼ tsp. garlic powder
4 egg whites, slightly
  beaten
3 Tbsp. olive oil
Green onion strips

Flatten chicken breasts between sheets of waxed paper. Mix bread crumbs, cheese, and 2 of the egg whites.

In separate bowl, stir together flour, wheat germ, salad dressing, oregano, and garlic powder. Beat remaining 2 egg whites in small dish.

Divide crumb mixture evenly atop chicken. Roll and secure with toothpicks. Dip chicken in egg whites, then in seasoned mixture. Brown in olive oil for 2 or 3 minutes. Place in baking dish coated with vegetable spray. Top with green onions. Bake for 20 to 30 minutes at 350°. Serves 6.

NUTRITIONAL INFORMATION

Calories	331	Sat. Fat (grams)	2.1 g
Total Fat	11 g	Cholesterol (mg)	72 mg
% Fat	30	Sodium (mg)	756 mg

Above figures based on per serving basis.

SOUTHERN CHICKEN BAKE

1 c. uncooked rice
1 c. sliced celery
1 c. chopped onions
2 tsp. parsley flakes
1 can condensed cream
of mushroom soup
¾ c. low-cal salad
dressing
1¼ c. water
4 skinned boneless
chicken breasts

Place rice in greased baking dish. Cover with combined vegetables and seasonings. Combine soup and salad dressing; add water to soup. Stir well. Pour half the soup mixture over vegetables. Top with chicken and remaining soup mixture. Salt and pepper; sprinkle with paprika. Bake for 1 hour at 350°. Serves 4.

NUTRITIONAL INFORMATION

Calories	507	Sat. Fat (grams)	3.2 g
Total Fat	16 g	Cholesterol (mg)	80 mg
% Fat	28	Sodium (mg)	1023 mg

Above figures based on per serving basis.

HEART HEALTHY TEXAS CHILI

2 lb. ground turkey meat
(24 oz. cooked)
1½ c. chopped onion
1 c. chopped green
pepper
3 cloves garlic, chopped
2 (28 oz.) cans low
sodium tomatoes in
puree (undrained),
chopped
2 c. water
1 (6 oz.) can low sodium
tomato paste
8 tsp. low sodium beef
bouillon
2 Tbsp. chili powder
1 Tbsp. ground cumin
2 tsp. oregano leaves
2 tsp. sugar
½ c. dried lentils
2 cans kidney beans,
drained and rinsed

In large kettle, brown turkey and pour off fat. Add onion, green pepper, and garlic. Cook and stir until tender. Add remaining ingredients. Cover. Bring to boil. Reduce heat and simmer for 1½ hours. Serves 12.

NUTRITIONAL INFORMATION

Calories	279	Sat. Fat (grams)	2.5 g
Total Fat	10 g	Cholesterol (mg)	62 mg
% Fat	30	Sodium (mg)	159 mg

Above figures based on per serving basis.

COUNTRY TURKEY

4 turkey fillets or skinned
chicken breasts
½ c. bread crumbs for
dredging, seasoned
with salt, pepper, and
garlic powder
2 Tbsp. olive oil or a
polyunsaturated oil
1 large onion, sliced
1 clove garlic, chopped
½ tsp. basil
¾ c. chicken stock

Roll the fillets in the heavily seasoned bread crumbs. Saute the onion in the oil until soft. Add the breaded fillets and saute over a moderate heat until they become deep golden. Turn the heat down to simmer. Add chicken stock (just about any liquid will work - be adventurous), garlic, and basil. Cover the pan and simmer for 15 to 20 minutes. Serve over rice and cover with the rich sauce that forms. Serves 4.

NUTRITIONAL INFORMATION

Calories	289	Sat. Fat (grams)	1.6 g
Total Fat	9 g	Cholesterol (mg)	96 mg
% Fat	29	Sodium (mg)	317 mg

Above figures based on per serving basis.

PIZZA OMELET

¾ c. pasteurized egg
substitute plus 5 egg
whites
½ c. sliced mushrooms
½ lb. skinless white meat
turkey, ground
(optional)
¼ lb. part-skim
Mozzarella cheese
4 Tbsp. chopped onion
4 Tbsp. chopped celery
4 Tbsp. chopped tomato
4 Tbsp. chopped green
pepper
½ tsp. garlic powder
½ tsp. oregano
½ tsp. basil
Paprika

Saute onion. Add meat. When mixture is cooked, add remaining vegetables and spices. Simmer for 2 minutes. Beat together eggs, shredded or chopped cheese, and 2 tablespoons water. Place vegetable mixture into a greased baking dish; pour the eggs over the top. Sprinkle with paprika. Bake for approximately 15 to 20 minutes at 450°. Serves 6.

NUTRITIONAL INFORMATION

Calories	144	Sat. Fat (grams)	2.4 g
Total Fat	5 g	Cholesterol (mg)	36 mg
% Fat	30	Sodium (mg)	223 mg

Above figures based on per serving basis.

SLOPPY TOMS

1 lb. skinless white meat
  turkey, ground
1 c. chopped onion
½ c. chopped celery
½ c. chopped green
  onion
½ c. chopped parsley
2 Tbsp. safflower oil
3 c. skim milk
2 Tbsp. cornstarch
1 Tbsp. fennel seed
½ tsp. cayenne pepper

Saute onion in oil. Add turkey and simmer until cooked. Add celery, fennel seed, and cayenne pepper. Stir in 2½ cups milk. Simmer. Mix cornstarch with ½ cup cold milk. Add to pan, stirring constantly. Add green onion and parsley. Heat through, but do not overcook. Serve over split buttermilk oat biscuits. Serves 6.

NUTRITIONAL INFORMATION			
Calories	197	Sat. Fat (grams)	0.8 g
Total Fat	6 g	Cholesterol (mg)	54 mg
% Fat	27	Sodium (mg)	111 mg

Above figures based on per serving basis.

TURKEY BURGERS

1 lb. skinless white meat
  turkey, ground
½ c. dried whole wheat
  bread crumbs
3 Tbsp. minced onion
2 garlic cloves, minced
1 Tbsp. lemon juice
1 tsp. Worcestershire
  sauce
1 tsp. low sodium soy
  sauce
½ tsp. paprika
¼ tsp. Tabasco
Freshly ground black
  pepper
2 tsp. mixed dried or
  fresh herbs (oregano,
  basil, thyme, chives,
  parsley, etc.)
6 whole wheat buns or
  pita bread

Combine all the ingredients. Shape the mixture into 6 patties. Broil, grill or cook the burgers in a nonstick pan until they are done. Serve on buns or in pita bread with tomatoes and lettuce. Makes 6 patties.

NUTRITIONAL INFORMATION			
Calories	284	Sat. Fat (grams)	2.5 g
Total Fat	10 g	Cholesterol (mg)	62 mg
% Fat	30	Sodium (mg)	444 mg

Above figures based on per serving basis.

TURKEY MEAT LOAF

1 lb. skinless white meat
  turkey, ground
1 egg white
½ c. oat bran
1 Tbsp. Worcestershire
  sauce
½ tsp. Dijon mustard
1 onion, chopped
½ green pepper
  (optional)
1 minced garlic clove
¼ tsp. sage
¼ tsp. pepper
¼ tsp. marjoram
¼ tsp. celery salt
4 Tbsp. chili sauce
Red pepper relish

Mix all ingredients, except red pepper relish, together and form into a loaf. Spread red pepper relish on top. Bake for 1¼ hours at 350°. Check with meat thermometer (170°) to be sure of doneness. Freezes well. Serves 4.

NUTRITIONAL INFORMATION			
Calories	195	Sat. Fat (grams)	0.5 g
Total Fat	2 g	Cholesterol (mg)	77 mg
% Fat	9	Sodium (mg)	432 mg

Above figures based on per serving basis.

TURKEY NOODLE TETRAZZINI

3 c. lowfat milk
1 crushed clove garlic
4 to 5 slices lowfat sharp
  Cheddar cheese
2 env. low salt chicken
  instant broth
½ bag no yolk noodles
2 c. turkey (or chicken)
½ c. low moisture, part-
  skim Mozzarella cheese
Pepper
Chives
Flour (to thicken)
8 oz. noodles

Cook noodles. Drain and put in large casserole dish (sprayed with vegetable cooking spray). Add turkey. Cook first 4 ingredients until cheese melts. Thicken slightly. Pour mixture over noodles and mix. Sprinkle Mozzarella cheese over top. Bake at 350° for 1 hour. Serves 6.

NUTRITIONAL INFORMATION			
Calories	281	Sat. Fat (grams)	5.1 g
Total Fat	9 g	Cholesterol (mg)	59 mg
% Fat	30	Sodium (mg)	305 mg

Above figures based on per serving basis.

CRISPY BAKED FISH

1 lb. fish fillets (fresh or
   frozen)
¼ tsp. salt (optional)
Dash of freshly ground
   pepper
1½ Tbsp. safflower or
   corn oil
⅓ c. corn flake crumbs

1. Wash and dry fillets; season.
2. Dip in oil; drain. Coat with corn flake crumbs. Arrange in either lightly oiled or Pam sprayed baking dish.
3. Bake at 350° for 30 minutes or until fish flakes. Serves 4.

NUTRITIONAL INFORMATION	
Calories..................166	Sat. Fat (grams).......0.6 g
Total Fat....................5 g	Cholesterol (mg).......49 mg
% Fat......................29	Sodium (mg)..........291 mg

Above figures based on per serving basis.

FILLETS IN LEMON

1 lb. firm orange roughy
   fillets
1 Tbsp. melted
   margarine
¼ c. parsley flakes
1 Tbsp. lemon juice
Paprika

In a 12x8x2 inch Pyrex pan, arrange fillets with thickest meaty areas to outside of pan. In small bowl, melt margarine. Add parsley flakes and lemon juice. Pour over fillets and sprinkle with paprika. Cover pan with plastic wrap, but leave corners open slightly. Microwave at HIGH for 8 minutes, rotating pan ½ turn after 5 minutes, until fish flakes easily with a fork. Serves 4.

NUTRITIONAL INFORMATION	
Calories..................118	Sat. Fat (grams).......0.5 g
Total Fat....................4 g	Cholesterol (mg).......26 mg
% Fat......................30	Sodium (mg)..........120 mg

Above figures based on per serving basis.

FISH ITALIAN

1 lb. fish (cod, etc.), cut
as desired
1½ Tbsp. corn or olive
oil
1 large onion, sliced or
chopped
1 large stalk celery,
chopped
½ green pepper, cut in 1
inch pieces
¼ tsp. garlic powder
¼ tsp. oregano
¼ tsp. rosemary
1 can tomato paste plus
1 or 2 Tbsp. water

Combine in microproof dish the oil, pepper, and celery. Cover and cook on HIGH for 5 minutes. Stir. Add all seasonings. Wash and dry fish; turn several times in dish to coat with oil and seasoning mix. Cover with tomato paste, mixed with water. Cover with wax paper. Microwave on HIGH for 6 minutes. (Can sprinkle Parmesan cheese on before or after if desired.) Serve over rice (brown preferred). Serves 4.

NUTRITIONAL INFORMATION			
Calories	193	Sat. Fat (grams)	0.9 g
Total Fat	6 g	Cholesterol (mg)	49 mg
% Fat	29	Sodium (mg)	407 mg

Above figures based on per serving basis.

GARLIC BROILED FISH FILLETS

1 lb. sole, flounder, or
cod
½ tsp. garlic powder
2 Tbsp. lemon or lime
juice
1 Tbsp. soft salt free
margarine
4 Tbsp. minced fresh
parsley (optional)

Combine garlic, juice, and margarine. Spread mixture over fish. Broil 3 to 4 inches from heat until fish flakes (5 to 8 minutes), depending on thickness of fish. Sprinkle with fresh parsley if desired. Serves 4.

NUTRITIONAL INFORMATION			
Calories	133	Sat. Fat (grams)	0.9 g
Total Fat	4 g	Cholesterol (mg)	54 mg
% Fat	30	Sodium (mg)	94 mg

Above figures based on per serving basis.

GRILLED SALMON WITH LIME BUTTER

2 Tbsp. freshly squeezed
   lime juice
2 tsp. mashed, pared
   ginger root
2 salmon fillets (¼ lb.
   each)
1 tsp. whipped diet
   margarine, softened
2 tsp. fresh grated lime
   peel
Lemon slices (garnish)
Lime slices (garnish)

In shallow bowl, combine lime juice and ginger root; add salmon fillets and let stand at room temperature for 15 minutes, turning fillets over every 5 minutes.

In small bowl, combine margarine and lime peel; cover and refrigerate until ready to serve. Preheat broiler. Spray nonstick baking sheet with nonstick cooking spray; arrange fillets on baking sheet. Broil until fish flakes easily when tested with a fork, about 2 minutes on each side.

To serve, on serving platter, arrange salmon fillets. Top each fillet with half the lime butter; garnish with lemon and lime slices. Serves 2.

NUTRITIONAL INFORMATION	
Calories.................146	Sat. Fat (grams).......0.8 g
Total Fat....................5 g	Cholesterol (mg).......59 mg
% Fat......................30	Sodium (mg)............85 mg

Above figures based on per serving basis.

ORANGE ROUGHY IN ORANGE-MINT-YOGURT SAUCE

1½ lb. orange roughy
   fillets
1 tsp. olive oil
½ tsp. minced ginger
   root
½ tsp. minced garlic
1 (8 oz.) ctn. plain nonfat
   yogurt
1 tsp. grated orange peel
1 tsp. minced fresh mint
   leaves
White pepper

Brush fish with oil and sprinkle lightly with ginger and garlic. Broil 3 to 4 inches from heat source for about 5 minutes or until fish flakes when tested with fork. Stir together yogurt, orange peel, and mint leaves. Season to taste with white pepper. To serve, spoon yogurt sauce over fish or serve separately. Serves 6.

NUTRITIONAL INFORMATION	
Calories.................117	Sat. Fat (grams)..........0 g
Total Fat....................2 g	Cholesterol (mg).......26 mg
% Fat......................14	Sodium (mg)..........110 mg

Above figures based on per serving basis.

SALMON PATTIES

1 (1 lb.) can salmon
4 egg whites or
pasteurized egg
substitute equal to 2
eggs
⅔ c. oat bran cereal
1 medium onion, minced
fine
1 Tbsp. finely chopped
parsley
1 Tbsp. fresh squeezed
lemon juice

Mix all ingredients together and make 8 patties shaped like hamburgers. Spray a nonstick pan with Pam and fry until crisp. Serves 8.

NUTRITIONAL INFORMATION	
Calories...................99	Sat. Fat (grams).......0.8 g
Total Fat...................3 g	Cholesterol (mg).......19 mg
% Fat.....................27	Sodium (mg)..........256 mg

Above figures based on per serving basis.

SCALLOPS AND VEGETABLES

2 Tbsp. finely chopped
white onion
2 Tbsp. diet margarine
2 c. thinly sliced
mushrooms
1 c. julienne carrots
1 c. julienne celery
1 Tbsp. chopped fresh
dill
¼ tsp. salt
Sprinkle of pepper
1 lb. sea scallops, halved
4 tsp. fresh lemon juice
Aluminum foil

Preheat oven to 350°. Saute onion in butter in large skillet for 1 minute. Add mushrooms, carrots, and celery. Cook, stirring constantly. Sprinkle with dill; salt and pepper. Set aside. Cut sheet of aluminum foil into 4 (12 inch) squares. Arrange scallops near middle of each sheet. Sprinkle with lemon juice, salt, and pepper. Top each with sauteed vegetables. Fold half of foil over to form triangle. Fold edges over twice to seal. Place package on cookie sheet. Bake for 15 minutes. Cut an "X" opening in package - eat as is! Serves 4.

NUTRITIONAL INFORMATION	
Calories.................157	Sat. Fat (grams).......0.6 g
Total Fat...................4 g	Cholesterol (mg).......37 mg
% Fat.....................22	Sodium (mg)..........382 mg

Above figures based on per serving basis.

BREADS, MUFFINS

ANGEL BISCUITS

1 pkg. yeast
¼ c. warm water
7 Tbsp. corn oil
4 c. self-rising flour
1 tsp. soda
½ c. sugar
1½ c. nonfat buttermilk

Dissolve yeast in warm water. Blend shortening and flour till evenly distributed. In separate bowl, mix soda, sugar, and buttermilk. Stir yeast and water in with buttermilk, then pour this mixture in with flour. Mix well. Roll out and cut or pat by hand to desired size. Place in greased pan and bake for 15 minutes at 400°. Makes 3 dozen.

Dough can be covered and kept in refrigerator for several days.

NUTRITIONAL INFORMATION			
Calories	88	Sat. Fat (grams)	0.4 g
Total Fat	3 g	Cholesterol (mg)	0 mg
% Fat	30	Sodium (mg)	222 mg

Above figures based on per serving basis.

BANANA BREAD

1½ c. all-purpose flour
½ c. sugar
2 tsp. baking powder
1 tsp. baking soda
½ tsp. salt
½ c. wheat germ or oat bran
3 medium ripe bananas, mashed (about 1 c.)
¼ c. buttermilk or plain yogurt
¼ c. corn oil
4 egg whites

Sift together the flour, sugar, baking powder, baking soda, and salt. Mix in the wheat germ or oat bran. Add all remaining ingredients and mix until well blended. Place in an oiled 8x4 inch loaf pan. Bake at 350° for 1 hour. Makes 1 loaf (16 slices).

Hint: You can freeze peeled ripe bananas and defrost as needed for bread and muffins.

NUTRITIONAL INFORMATION			
Calories	134	Sat. Fat (grams)	0.6 g
Total Fat	4 g	Cholesterol (mg)	0 mg
% Fat	26	Sodium (mg)	225 mg

Above figures based on per serving basis.

CORN BREAD

1 c. sifted all-purpose
flour
½ tsp. salt (optional)
2 tsp. baking powder
¾ c. corn meal
1 c. skim milk
2 egg whites (or ¼ c.
pasteurized egg
substitute)
⅓ c. corn syrup (or
sugar)
¼ c. vegetable oil

1. Sift dry ingredients together. Mix in liquid ingredients.
2. Pour into 8 inch square pan, which has been oiled or sprayed with cooking spray.
3. Bake at 425° until golden brown. Makes 8 inch square or round pan. Serves 8.

NUTRITIONAL INFORMATION

Calories	218	Sat. Fat (grams)	0.6 g
Total Fat	7 g	Cholesterol (mg)	1 mg
% Fat	29	Sodium (mg)	302 mg

Above figures based on per serving basis.

MEXICAN CORN BREAD

3 egg whites
8 oz. fat free yogurt
1 small can creamed
corn
2½ Tbsp. corn oil
1½ c. yellow corn meal
3 tsp. baking powder
1 tsp. salt
2 chopped jalapeno
peppers (seeds
removed)
2 Tbsp. chopped green
pepper
1 c. grated Mozzarella
cheese

Mix all ingredients in order given. Bake at 350° for 30 to 45 minutes in a well greased iron skillet. Serves 8.

NUTRITIONAL INFORMATION

Calories	218	Sat. Fat (grams)	2.2 g
Total Fat	7 g	Cholesterol (mg)	8 mg
% Fat	30	Sodium (mg)	653 mg

Above figures based on per serving basis.

CORN MEAL PANCAKES

1 c. boiling water
¾ c. yellow corn meal
1¼ c. lowfat buttermilk,
    soy milk or sour skim
    milk*
1 whole egg plus 1 egg
    white or 3 egg whites,
    lightly beaten
1 c. sifted whole wheat
    flour
1 Tbsp. baking powder
½ tsp. salt
¼ tsp. soda
⅛ c. safflower oil

Pour boiling water over corn meal. Stir until thick. Add milk and stir in eggs. Sift together flour, baking powder, salt, and soda. Add to corn meal mixture. Stir in oil. Use ¼ cup batter per cake. Pour on hot, ungreased griddle. When surface bubbles, turn and cook other side until lightly browned. Makes 14 pancakes.

*To make sour milk, add 1 tablespoon lemon juice or vinegar per 1 cup milk.

NUTRITIONAL INFORMATION	
Calories.................89	Sat. Fat (grams).......0.5 g
Total Fat..................3 g	Cholesterol (mg).......16 mg
% Fat.....................27	Sodium (mg).........235 mg

Above figures based on per serving basis.

DATE NUT BREAD

3 pasteurized egg
    substitutes
1 c. sugar
1 tsp. vanilla
1 c. all-purpose flour
1 pkg. chopped dates
1⅓ c. chopped nuts

Beat eggs and sugar together. Add vanilla, then flour. Stir in fruit and nuts till thoroughly blended. Bake at 325° for 1 hour in greased and floured loaf pans. Makes 16 servings.

NUTRITIONAL INFORMATION	
Calories.................190	Sat. Fat (grams).......0.7 g
Total Fat..................7 g	Cholesterol (mg).........0 mg
% Fat.....................30	Sodium (mg).........23 mg

Above figures based on per serving basis.

PUMPKIN LOAF

¾ c. cooked, mashed
  pumpkin
⅓ c. firmly packed
  brown sugar
1½ tsp. vanilla extract
1 egg
1¾ c. all-purpose flour
¾ tsp. baking powder
½ tsp. baking soda
¼ tsp. salt
1 tsp. ground cinnamon
½ tsp. ground nutmeg
¼ tsp. ground allspice
¼ tsp. ground ginger
¾ c. skim milk
3 Tbsp. vegetable oil
Vegetable cooking spray

Beat pumpkin, sugar, and vanilla at medium speed of an electric mixer for 1 minute; add egg and beat well. Sift together flour and next 7 ingredients. Add pumpkin mixture alternately with milk and oil, mixing well at low speed. Pour batter into two 5 x 2½ inch loaf pans coated with cooking spray. Bake at 350° for 45 minutes or until a wooden pick inserted in center comes out clean. Cool for 10 minutes; remove from pans and cool completely on a wire rack. Makes 2 loaves, 32 servings.

NUTRITIONAL INFORMATION

Calories	49	Sat. Fat (grams)	0 g
Total Fat	2 g	Cholesterol (mg)	7 mg
% Fat	28	Sodium (mg)	54 mg

Above figures based on per serving basis.

SOUR CREAM COFFEECAKE

3½ Tbsp. corn oil
¼ c. liquid margarine
1½ c. sugar
2 pasteurized egg
  substitutes
1 c. light sour cream
1 tsp. vanilla
2 c. all-purpose flour
1 tsp. baking powder
1 tsp. soda
½ c. brown sugar
1 tsp. cinnamon
1¼ c. powdered sugar
3 Tbsp. skim milk
⅓ c. chopped nuts

Cream oil, margarine, and sugar. Add egg substitutes, sour cream, and vanilla. Combine flour, baking powder, and baking soda. Add gradually to sugar and oil mixture. Place batter in coffee cake pan or two 8 inch round cake pans.

Mix brown sugar and cinnamon, then sprinkle on top of batter. Bake at 350° for 30 minutes. Remove from oven and cover with glaze of powdered sugar and milk. Sprinkle with chopped nuts. Serves 16.

NUTRITIONAL INFORMATION

Calories	280	Sat. Fat (grams)	2.2 g
Total Fat	10 g	Cholesterol (mg)	6 mg
% Fat	30	Sodium (mg)	161 mg

Above figures based on per serving basis.

APPLE CINNAMON MUFFINS

2¼ c. oat bran cereal
¼ c. brown sugar
1¼ tsp. cinnamon
1 Tbsp. baking powder
¼ c. chopped walnuts
¼ c. raisins
½ c. skim milk or
   evaporated skim milk
¾ c. frozen apple juice
   concentrate
2 egg whites
2 Tbsp. vegetable oil
1 medium apple, cored
   and chopped

Preheat the oven to 425°. Mix the dry ingredients in a large bowl. Mix the milk, apple juice concentrate, egg whites, and the oil. Add the walnuts, raisins, and apples. Line the muffin pans with paper baking cups; fill with batter. Bake for 13 to 15 minutes. Test for doneness with toothpick. After cooling, store in a plastic bag to retain moisture and softness. Serve with applesauce or with apple butter. Makes 12 muffins.

NUTRITIONAL INFORMATION

Calories	144	Sat. Fat (grams)	0.6 g
Total Fat	5 g	Cholesterol (mg)	0 mg
% Fat	27	Sodium (mg)	143 mg

Above figures based on per serving basis.

BANANA BRAN MUFFINS

1 c. all-purpose flour
1 tsp. baking powder
1 tsp. baking soda
1 egg, beaten
¾ c. lowfat milk
2 Tbsp. diet margarine
6 packets sugar
   substitute
1½ c. bran cereal
½ c. mashed banana
1 Tbsp. honey

Preheat oven to 400°. Spray 12 muffin pan cups with nonstick cooking spray. In separate bowl, blend egg, milk, margarine, and sugar substitute. Stir bran cereal. Let stand for 5 minutes. Mix mashed banana with honey until well mixed. Add to bran mixture. Stir in flour mixture just until well blended. Do not overmix. Fill muffin cups ⅔ full. Bake for 18 to 20 minutes, or until toothpick comes out clean. Let stand for 2 to 3 minutes. Remove to wire rack to cool. Makes 12 muffins.

NUTRITIONAL INFORMATION

Calories	105	Sat. Fat (grams)	0.6 g
Total Fat	2 g	Cholesterol (mg)	19 mg
% Fat	17	Sodium (mg)	292 mg

Above figures based on per serving basis.

BLUEBERRY MUFFINS

½ c. corn oil
1½ c. sugar
3 egg whites
½ c. skim milk
2 c. flour
2 tsp. baking powder
½ tsp. salt
1¾ c. blueberries (fresh or frozen)

Cream oil and sugar; add egg whites and mix well. Blend in milk. Combine dry ingredients; mix by hand into the first mixture. Fold in blueberries very gently.

Fill muffin tins to the top. Sprinkle each muffin with sugar and bake for 30 minutes till golden brown at 375°. Makes 12 muffins.

NUTRITIONAL INFORMATION

Calories	273	Sat. Fat (grams)	1.3 g
Total Fat	9 g	Cholesterol (mg)	0 mg
% Fat	30	Sodium (mg)	191 mg

Above figures based on per serving basis.

BLUEBERRY OAT BRAN MUFFINS

2 c. oat bran
¼ c. brown sugar
¼ c. chopped pecans
2 tsp. baking powder
½ tsp. salt
¼ c. applesauce
½ c. skim milk
1 egg and 1 egg white, beaten
¼ c. honey
½ c. fresh or frozen blueberries

Preheat oven to 425°. Line a 12 cup muffin tin with paper liners or spray with vegetable spray. Combine oat bran, brown sugar, pecans, baking powder, and salt. Mix applesauce, milk, eggs, and honey. Add this mixture to the bran mixture, stirring the ingredients just enough to combine them. Fold in blueberries. Fill muffin tins and bake for 15 minutes, or until they are lightly browned. Remove them to a rack to cool down. Makes 12 muffins.

NUTRITIONAL INFORMATION

Calories	105	Sat. Fat (grams)	0.5 g
Total Fat	3 g	Cholesterol (mg)	18 mg
% Fat	22	Sodium (mg)	188 mg

Above figures based on per serving basis.

DESSERTS

AUTUMN OUTING ORANGE CAKE

2 large eggs
1½ c. granulated sugar
½ c. softened diet
   margarine
2½ c. all-purpose flour
1 (10¾ oz.) can tomato
   soup
4 tsp. baking powder
1 tsp. baking soda
½ tsp. ginger
½ tsp. nutmeg
½ tsp. cinnamon
¼ c. orange marmalade
1 c. confectioners sugar

Heat oven to 350°. Grease and flour two 9 inch round cake pans. Mix with electric mixer at medium speed the eggs, sugar, margarine, flour, ¼ cup water, baking powder, baking soda, ginger, nutmeg, and cinnamon for about 3 minutes. When all is blended well, pour into pans. Bake for 25 to 30 minutes until wooden pick inserted in center comes out clean. Cool layers. Place one layer on plate. Spread with orange marmalade. Place other layer on top. Mix 2 tablespoons of water into confectioners sugar. Stir until smooth. Drizzle over cake. Serves 12.

NUTRITIONAL INFORMATION

Calories	322	Sat. Fat (grams)	1.2 g
Total Fat	6 g	Cholesterol (mg)	35 mg
% Fat	18	Sodium (mg)	506 mg

Above figures based on per serving basis.

CARROT CAKE

¾ c. sugar
1 c. grated carrots
1 c. raisins
1 tsp. cinnamon
1 tsp. grated nutmeg
1 tsp. ground cloves
1½ c. water
2½ Tbsp. margarine
2 c. flour
2 tsp. baking soda
¼ tsp. salt
1 c. chopped walnuts

Preheat oven to 325°. Grease a 9x13 inch baking pan with margarine. In a small saucepan, combine sugar, carrots, raisins, cinnamon, nutmeg, cloves, water, and margarine. Bring to a boil. Reduce heat and simmer for 5 minutes. Pour into mixing bowl and cool to lukewarm. Add flour, baking soda, and salt. Mix well. Stir in walnuts. Pour into baking pan and bake for 40 minutes. Makes 24 slices.

NUTRITIONAL INFORMATION

Calories	128	Sat. Fat (grams)	0.5 g
Total Fat	4 g	Cholesterol (mg)	0 mg
% Fat	30	Sodium (mg)	144 mg

Above figures based on per serving basis.

CHOCOLATE ANGEL CAKE

¾ c. sifted cake flour
¼ c. cocoa
1½ c. sugar
1½ c. (12) egg whites
1½ tsp. cream of tartar
1½ tsp. vanilla

Sift flour, cocoa, and ¾ cup sugar 4 times. Beat egg whites with cream of tartar and vanilla till stiff enough to form soft peaks, but still moist and glossy. Add the remaining ¾ cup sugar, 2 tablespoons at a time, continuing to beat until meringue holds stiff peak. Sift about ¼ cup of the flour-cocoa mixture over whites and fold in. Blend in remaining flour-cocoa by fourths. Bake in ungreased 10 inch tube pan in moderate oven (375°) for 35 to 40 minutes or till done. Invert pan and let cool. Serves 16.

NUTRITIONAL INFORMATION	
Calories.................106	Sat. Fat (grams).........0 g
Total Fat......less than 1 g	Cholesterol (mg).........0 mg
% Fat.......................2	Sodium (mg)............42 mg

Above figures based on per serving basis.

CINNAMON CAKE

½ c. vegetable oil
1½ c. sugar
½ c. orange juice
1 Tbsp. orange peel
½ c. white raisins
½ c. dark raisins
¼ c. chopped walnuts
3 c. flour
2 tsp. baking powder
1 tsp. baking soda
1 tsp. cinnamon

Beat oil, sugar, and orange juice. Add orange peel, raisins, and walnuts. Add flour, baking powder, soda, and cinnamon. Beat well with wooden spoon. Bake at 350° in greased 10 inch tube pan for about 1 hour. Top with confectioners sugar when done. Serves 16.

NUTRITIONAL INFORMATION	
Calories.................266	Sat. Fat (grams).......0.6 g
Total Fat..................8 g	Cholesterol (mg).........0 mg
% Fat.....................27	Sodium (mg).........142 mg

Above figures based on per serving basis.

WONDERFUL GINGERBREAD

2 c. flour
½ c. sugar
1½ tsp. ginger
½ tsp. cinnamon
2 tsp. baking powder
Scant 1 tsp. soda
¼ tsp. salt
¾ c. molasses
1 c. nonfat buttermilk
1 pasteurized egg
   substitute
¼ c. liquid margarine
1 to 2 tsp. vanilla

Place all dry ingredients in sifter. Place wet ingredients in mixing bowl. Sift dry ingredients in the mixing bowl and beat till smooth. Pour into greased 9x5x3 inch loaf pan. Bake for about 1 hour at 350°. Serves 16.

NUTRITIONAL INFORMATION		
Calories................159	Sat. Fat (grams).......0.6 g	
Total Fat...................3 g	Cholesterol (mg).........1 mg	
% Fat......................19	Sodium (mg)..........230 mg	

Above figures based on per serving basis.

LEMONY ANGEL CAKE

This light-as-a-feather, luscious cake is surprisingly low in cholesterol as well as in calories. Angel food cake itself is both fat and cholesterol free, as is the pudding mix. The extremely modest 2 milligrams of cholesterol comes from the dairy products. This company dessert can be made the day before serving and refrigerated.

1 (about 16 oz.) box
   white angel food cake
   mix

Double Lemon Filling:
1 (4 serving size) pkg.
   sugar free instant
   lemon pudding and pie
   filling
2 c. cold skim milk
1 (8 oz.) container lemon
   lowfat yogurt
2 env. (1 (2.8 oz.) box)
   whipped topping mix
Thin lemon rounds,
   halved, and fresh mint
   leaves for garnish

Prepare cake mix; bake and cool following package directions.

Filling: At least 1 hour before using, beat pudding mix and skim milk according to package directions. Fold in lemon yogurt until blended. Cover and refrigerate for at least 1 hour, until mixture is of spreading consistency.

Meanwhile, beat topping mix as directed on label, using cold skim milk instead of whole milk.

To assemble, slice cake horizontally into 3 layers. Put 1 layer on serving plate. Spread with ½ filling. Repeat with second layer and remaining filling. Top with last layer. Frost top and sides with the whipped topping. Garnish just before serving. Serves 12.

NUTRITIONAL INFORMATION		
Calories................218	Sat. Fat (grams).......2.7 g	
Total Fat...................3 g	Cholesterol (mg).........2 mg	
% Fat......................13	Sodium (mg)..........432 mg	

Above figures based on per serving basis.

FLORIDA CHEESECAKE

3 c. low fat creamed
  cottage cheese
1 c. pure maple syrup
1 c. plain yogurt
6 Tbsp. fresh lime juice
2 eggs, well beaten
2 env. plain gelatin
1 c. stiffly whipped
  cream
Graham cracker crumbs

Combine syrup, yogurt, eggs, and gelatin in top of double boiler. Stir constantly over medium heat until gelatin is dissolved. Using a blender or rotary beater, blend cottage cheese with lime juice until smooth. Combine cheese with gelatin mixture and blend well. Fold in the whipping cream. Pour into a greased springform pan, which has been buttered and dusted with graham crumbs. Chill until set. Serves 12.

NUTRITIONAL INFORMATION	
Calories.................186	Sat. Fat (grams).......3.7 g
Total Fat...................6 g	Cholesterol (mg).......56 mg
% Fat......................30	Sodium (mg)..........258 mg

Above figures based on per serving basis.

REFRIGERATOR PINEAPPLE CHEESE CAKE

¾ c. graham cracker
  crumbs
2 Tbsp. melted
  margarine
1 Tbsp. oil
1 (3 oz.) pkg. pineapple
  gelatin (can use low
  calorie type)
1 c. boiling water
1½ lb. lowfat cottage
  cheese
¼ c. sugar
½ tsp. salt
1 (8½ oz.) can crushed
  pineapple in juice
  (undrained)
1 Tbsp. cornstarch
2 tsp. water

Combine first 3 ingredients. Press into bottom of an 8 inch spring form pan. Chill. Dissolve gelatin in boiling water. Cool to lukewarm.

In blender, combine cheese, sugar, and salt. Blend until completely smooth with no lumps. Slowly add gelatin and blend well. Pour mix into chilled crust and refrigerate until firm. Bring pineapple, water, and cornstarch to a boil in saucepan, stirring constantly. Cool for 15 minutes. Spread on cake. Chill for 1 hour. Serves 12.

NUTRITIONAL INFORMATION	
Calories.................167	Sat. Fat (grams).......1.3 g
Total Fat...................5 g	Cholesterol (mg).........5 mg
% Fat......................26	Sodium (mg)..........405 mg

Above figures based on per serving basis.

REFRIGERATOR STRAWBERRY CHEESE CAKE

1 c. graham cracker
crumbs
2 Tbsp. margarine,
melted
1 Tbsp. oil
1 (3 oz.) pkg. strawberry
gelatin
1 c. boiling water
1½ lb. lowfat cottage
cheese
¼ c. sugar
½ tsp. salt
10 medium strawberries

Combine first 3 ingredients. Press onto the bottom of an 8 inch spring form pan. Chill. Dissolve the gelatin in the boiling water and cool to lukewarm.

In a blender, thoroughly mix the cheese, sugar, and salt. Slowly add the gelatin and blend well. Slice or mash the strawberries. Pour over the top. Chill for at least 1 hour. Serves 12.

NUTRITIONAL INFORMATION	
Calories 171	Sat. Fat (grams) .... 1.3 g
Total Fat .... 5 g	Cholesterol (mg) .... 5 mg
% Fat 27	Sodium (mg) .... 420 mg

Above figures based on per serving basis.

BANANA BARS

⅓ c. margarine
½ c. honey
1 egg
1 tsp. vanilla
2 medium size ripe
bananas, mashed
1½ c. whole wheat flour
1½ tsp. baking powder
½ tsp. salt

Preheat oven to 350°. Beat together margarine and honey. Add egg and vanilla; beat well. Stir in mashed bananas. Stir together flour, baking powder, and salt. Add to the banana mixture and beat until combined. Spread evenly in a greased 8 inch square pan. Bake for 20 minutes. Cool and cut into bars. Makes 20 bars.

NUTRITIONAL INFORMATION	
Calories 98	Sat. Fat (grams) .... 0.6 g
Total Fat .... 4 g	Cholesterol (mg) .... 11 mg
% Fat 30	Sodium (mg) .... 130 mg

Above figures based on per serving basis.

BLACK FOREST BARS

⅓ c. margarine, softened
¾ c. plus 2 Tbsp. sugar, divided
4 egg whites or ⅔ c. frozen pasteurized egg substitute, thawed
1¼ tsp. vanilla extract, divided
⅔ c. all-purpose flour
⅓ c. unsweetened cocoa
½ tsp. baking powder
¼ tsp. salt
Vegetable cooking spray
1 (20 oz.) can reduced-calorie cherry fruit pie filling
2 egg whites
⅛ tsp. cream of tartar

Cream margarine; gradually add ¾ cup sugar, beating well at medium speed of an electric mixer. Add 4 egg whites and 1 teaspoon vanilla; beat well. Combine flour and next 3 ingredients; add to sugar mixture and stir well.

Spread batter into a 13x9x2 inch baking pan coated with cooking spray. Bake at 325° for 18 minutes or until a wooden pick inserted in center comes out clean. Cool completely in pan on a wire rack. Spread pie filling evenly over cake.

Beat 2 egg whites (at room temperature) and cream of tartar at high speed of an electric mixer until soft peaks form. Gradually add remaining 2 tablespoons sugar, one tablespoon at a time, beating until stiff peaks form. Fold in remaining ¼ teaspoon vanilla. Spoon mixture into decorating bag fitted with a large star tip; pipe 16 meringue dollops onto pie filling. Bake at 450° for 8 minutes or until meringue is lightly browned. Serves 16.

NUTRITIONAL INFORMATION	
Calories 135	Sat. Fat (grams) .... 0.8 g
Total Fat .... 4 g	Cholesterol (mg) .... 0 mg
% Fat 28	Sodium (mg) .... 118 mg

Above figures based on per serving basis.

BUTTERSCOTCH BROWNIES

3 Tbsp. oil
1 c. light brown sugar, firmly packed
2 egg whites, slightly beaten
¾ c. sifted flour
1 tsp. baking powder
½ tsp. salt
½ tsp. vanilla extract

Preheat oven to 375°. Blend oil and sugar. Stir in beaten egg whites. Sift flour, baking powder, and salt together; combine with egg mixture. Add vanilla to the batter; spread in an oiled 8x8x2 inch pan and bake for 25 minutes. Do not overbake. Cool slightly and cut into squares. Makes 16 squares.

NUTRITIONAL INFORMATION	
Calories 81	Sat. Fat (grams) .... 0 g
Total Fat .... 3 g	Cholesterol (mg) .... 0 mg
% Fat 29	Sodium (mg) .... 108 mg

Above figures based on per serving basis.

CHEWY OATMEAL COOKIES

¼ c. tub margarine
¼ c. brown sugar,
  packed
1 egg, slightly beaten
1½ tsp. vanilla
½ c. whole wheat flour
¾ tsp. baking powder
1 c. wheat germ
2 c. rolled oats
½ c. raisins
1 Tbsp. water

Cream together margarine and sugar. Add egg and vanilla. Beat well. Stir together remaining dry ingredients and combine with creamed mixture and water. Stir until well blended.

Drop by teaspoonfuls onto greased cookie sheet. Flatten slightly. Bake in preheated 375° oven for 9 to 12 minutes. Makes 6 dozen (1 inch) cookies.

NUTRITIONAL INFORMATION	
Calories...................29	Sat. Fat (grams)..........0 g
Total Fat...................1 g	Cholesterol (mg)..........3 mg
% Fat......................30	Sodium (mg)............12 mg

Above figures based on per serving basis.

CHOCOLATE CHIP COOKIES

2 c. flour
1 tsp. baking soda
½ tsp. salt
2 egg whites
3 Tbsp. water
1 tsp. vanilla
1 c. firmly packed brown
  sugar
¼ c. vegetable oil
½ c. semi-sweet
  chocolate chips

1. Heat oven to 375°. Spray baking sheets with vegetable pan spray.
2. Combine flour, soda, and salt; set aside.
3. Combine egg whites, water, and vanilla; set aside.
4. Blend brown sugar and vegetable oil in large bowl at low speed. Add egg mixture. Beat until smooth. Add flour mixture in 3 parts at lowest speed. Scrape bowl well after each addition. Stir in chocolate chips.
5. Drop dough by rounded teaspoonfuls onto baking sheet.
6. Bake at 375° for 7 to 8 minutes or until lightly browned. Cool on baking sheets for 1 minute. Remove to cooling rack. Makes 36 cookies.

NUTRITIONAL INFORMATION	
Calories...................66	Sat. Fat (grams).......0.5 g
Total Fat...................2 g	Cholesterol (mg).........0 mg
% Fat......................30	Sodium (mg)............70 mg

Above figures based on per serving basis.

BROWNIE CRINKLES

1 pkg. low-fat fudge
   brownie mix
¼ c. water
¼ c. fat-free cholesterol-
   free pasteurized egg
   product or 1 egg
½ c. powdered sugar

Heat oven to 350°. Grease cookie sheet. Mix brownie mix (dry), water and egg product about 50 strokes or until well blended. Shape dough by rounded teaspoonfuls into balls. Roll in powdered sugar. Place balls about 2 inches apart on cookie sheet.

Bake 10 to 12 minutes or until almost no indentation remains when touched lightly in center. Immediately remove from cookie sheet. Cool on wire rack. Makes 3½ dozen cookies.

NUTRITIONAL INFORMATION			
Calories	61	Sat. Fat (grams)	0.4 g
Total Fat	1 g	Cholesterol (mg)	0 mg
% Fat	15	Sodium (mg)	51 mg

Above figures based on per serving basis.

GINGER SNAPS

6 Tbsp. corn oil
1 c. sugar
1 egg white
1 Tbsp. molasses
2 c. all-purpose flour
2 tsp. baking soda
1 tsp. ginger
1 tsp. cinnamon
Dash of salt

In large bowl, mix oil, sugar, egg white, and molasses. In separate bowl, sift flour, soda, ginger, cinnamon, and salt. Add to oil-sugar mixture and blend well. Roll into log shaped roll, wrap in waxed paper, and freeze.

These may be sliced and baked when desired. Place on greased cookie sheet and bake for 10 to 12 minutes at 350°. Makes 5 dozen cookies.

NUTRITIONAL INFORMATION			
Calories	42	Sat. Fat (grams)	0.2 g
Total Fat	1 g	Cholesterol (mg)	0 mg
% Fat	30	Sodium (mg)	44 mg

Above figures based on per serving basis.

OLD-FASHIONED SUGAR COOKIES

6½ Tbsp. corn oil
1 c. sugar
2 egg whites
1 tsp. vanilla extract
¼ tsp. almond extract
2¾ c. all-purpose flour
¾ tsp. salt
½ tsp. baking powder
½ tsp. baking soda

Cream oil and sugar; add egg whites, vanilla, and almond. Blend well. Combine dry ingredients and add to first mixture. Wrap in plastic wrap and place in refrigerator overnight. Roll on floured surface and cut in desired shapes. If desired, brush egg white on cookies and sprinkle with colored sugar before baking.

These cookies also may be shaped by rolling in 1 inch balls and flattened with a glass bottom dipped in sugar. These are like old-fashioned tea cakes. Bake at 350° for about 7 minutes. Makes 3-4 dozen cookies.

NUTRITIONAL INFORMATION			
Calories	79	Sat. Fat (grams)	0.3 g
Total Fat	3 g	Cholesterol (mg)	0 mg
% Fat	29	Sodium (mg)	72 mg

Above figures based on per serving basis.

PUMPKIN COOKIES

½ c. margarine
1 c. brown sugar
1 c. pumpkin
1 egg or substitute
   equivalent
1 tsp. vanilla
2 c. flour
1 tsp. soda
1 tsp. baking powder
1 tsp. cinnamon
½ tsp. salt
½ c. nuts
1 c. dates or raisins

Frosting:
1 Tbsp. margarine
2 c. powdered sugar
2 Tbsp. evaporated milk
1 tsp. vanilla

Cream margarine and brown sugar. Mix in pumpkin, egg or pasteurized egg substitute, and vanilla. Add dry ingredients gradually, mixing well. Stir in nuts and dates or raisins. Drop by spoonfuls onto cookie sheet. Bake at 350° until brown, about 10 minutes. Makes 2 dozen cookies.

Frosting: Melt margarine and combine with other ingredients. Frost cookies. (Add orange food coloring as desired.)

NUTRITIONAL INFORMATION			
Calories	184	Sat. Fat (grams)	1 g
Total Fat	6 g	Cholesterol (mg)	9 mg
% Fat	30	Sodium (mg)	175 mg

Above figures based on per serving basis.

CHOCOLATE CHESS PIE

1 (9 inch) pie shell
  (unbaked)
1½ c. sugar
3 Tbsp. cocoa
⅛ c. liquid margarine
2 pasteurized egg
  substitutes
⅛ tsp. salt
1 (5 oz.) can evaporated
  skim milk
1 tsp. vanilla

Prepare unbaked pie shell. Mix sugar, cocoa, and margarine. Stir well. Add eggs and beat with electric mixer. Add salt, milk, and vanilla. Pour filling into pie shell. Bake at 350° for 35 to 45 minutes. Serves 8.

NUTRITIONAL INFORMATION		
Calories.................322	Sat. Fat (grams).......3.7 g	
Total Fat................11 g	Cholesterol (mg).........8 mg	
% Fat.....................30	Sodium (mg)..........198 mg	

Above figures based on per serving basis.

LIME PIE

Crust:
1 c. fresh whole wheat
  bread crumbs
⅔ c. finely chopped
  walnuts, pecans or
  almonds
2 Tbsp. egg whites
2 Tbsp. frozen
  unsweetened apple
  juice concentrate
½ tsp. ground cinnamon
½ tsp. nutmeg

Filling:
½ c. frozen apple juice
  concentrate, defrosted
1 env. unflavored gelatin
⅓ c. honey
1 Tbsp. grated lime rind
⅓ c. fresh lime juice
¼ tsp. vanilla
1½ c. (12 oz.) plain fat
  free yogurt

Preheat oven to 375°. Combine all crust ingredients in a bowl. Oil a 9 inch springform pan or pie pan. Press the mixture into the bottom and sides of the pan. Bake for 6 to 8 minutes or until firm. Let cool while making the filling.

Filling: Put the apple juice concentrate in a small saucepan. Sprinkle the gelatin over the concentrate and let stand for a few minutes. Heat the mixture over low heat until the gelatin dissolves. Pour into a bowl. Add the honey, 2 teaspoons of the rind, lime juice, and vanilla. Chill in the freezer or refrigerator until it is the consistency of raw egg whites. With an electric mixer, whip the lime mixture until fluffy. Stir in the yogurt and whip again. Pour into the prepared crust. Sprinkle the remaining lime rind over the top and chill the pie until firm. To serve, remove springform pan ring if used or slice directly from pie pan. Serves 8.

NUTRITIONAL INFORMATION		
Calories.................194	Sat. Fat (grams).......0.7 g	
Total Fat................7 g	Cholesterol (mg).........1 mg	
% Fat.....................29	Sodium (mg)..........84 mg	

Above figures based on per serving basis.

PUMPKIN PIE

1 (16 oz.) can pumpkin
½ c. light brown sugar
¼ c. sugar
1 tsp. cinnamon
½ tsp. ginger
½ tsp. salt
2 pasteurized egg
  substitutes
1½ c. evaporated skim
  milk
1 (9 inch) unbaked pie
  shell

Blend all ingredients in large mixing bowl with electric mixer. Pour into an unbaked pie shell. Bake at 425° for 15 minutes, then reduce heat to 350° and bake for 45 minutes. Test for doneness by inserting knife into center of filling. Serves 8.

NUTRITIONAL INFORMATION

Calories	247	Sat. Fat (grams)	3.1 g
Total Fat	8 g	Cholesterol (mg)	9 mg
% Fat	28	Sodium (mg)	311 mg

Above figures based on per serving basis.

BAKED PUMPKIN PIE

1 (9 inch) pie shell
  (unbaked)
⅔ c. granulated sugar
⅛ tsp. salt
½ tsp. cinnamon
½ tsp. ginger
½ tsp. nutmeg
Pinch of ground cloves
1½ c. canned pumpkin
1 tsp. vanilla extract
1½ c. evaporated skim
  milk
½ tsp. orange rind
3 egg whites, slightly
  beaten

Preheat oven to 450°. Combine the sugar, salt, cinnamon, ginger, nutmeg, and cloves. Stir in the pumpkin. Add the vanilla, evaporated skim milk, orange rind, and egg whites. Beat with an electric mixer until smooth.

Pour into the unbaked pie shell and bake for 10 minutes at 450°. Reduce heat to 325° and bake until a knife inserted in the filling comes out clean, about 45 minutes. Serves 8.

NUTRITIONAL INFORMATION

Calories	245	Sat. Fat (grams)	3.1 g
Total Fat	8 g	Cholesterol (mg)	9 mg
% Fat	27	Sodium (mg)	200 mg

Above figures based on per serving basis.

SWEET CHERRY CREAM PIE

8 oz. fat free cream
 cheese, softened
1 small can evaporated
 milk
3 Tbsp. honey
1 can dark sweet cherries
 packed in juice or
 water
1 Tbsp. lemon juice
1 tsp. vanilla or almond
 extract
1 env. plain gelatin
1 graham cracker crust

In a small saucepan, bring liquid from cherries to a boil. Add honey. Dissolve gelatin in juice. Add remaining ingredients, except for cherries. Beat well. Add most of fruit, reserving several pieces for garnish. Pour mixture in prepared pie shell and chill. Top with halved cherries, cut side down. Serves 8.

NUTRITIONAL INFORMATION

Calories...............210	Sat. Fat (grams).......1.5 g
Total Fat...................6 g	Cholesterol (mg).........3 mg
% Fat.....................26	Sodium (mg)..........283 mg

Above figures based on per serving basis.

STRAWBERRY PIE

1 (9 inch) baked pie shell
¾ c. sugar
2 Tbsp. cornstarch
2 Tbsp. corn syrup
1 c. water
2 Tbsp. strawberry
 gelatin powder
1 qt. fresh whole
 strawberries, trimmed
 and washed

Crumb Pie Crust:
1 c. dry crumbs made
 from Melba toast,
 graham crackers, corn
 flakes, or other crisp
 cereal
¼ c. sugar
2 Tbsp. oil
¼ tsp. cinnamon

Filling: Mix the sugar, cornstarch, syrup, and water together. Bring to a boil and cook until thick and clear. Add the gelatin powder, stirring until dissolved. Cool. Arrange the whole strawberries to cover the bottom of the baked pie shell. Pour the gelatin mixture over the strawberries and chill until set. Serves 8.

Crumb Pie Crust: Toss ingredients until crumbs are well moistened with oil. Press carefully into a pie pan, covering bottom and sides. Bake at 375° for 10 minutes.

NUTRITIONAL INFORMATION

Calories...............364	Sat. Fat (grams).......3.6 g
Total Fat.................13 g	Cholesterol (mg).........7 mg
% Fat.....................30	Sodium (mg)..........195 mg

Above figures based on per serving basis.

STRAWBERRY CHIFFON PIE

1½ c. strawberries
½ c. sugar
1 env. gelatin (1 Tbsp.)
¼ c. sugar
¾ c. water
1 Tbsp. lemon juice
⅛ tsp. salt
2 egg whites
1 (9 inch) baked pie shell
or crumb crust

Wash and hull strawberries. Save a few perfect berries to garnish the finished pie. Slice the rest and cover with ½ cup sugar. Let stand for ½ hour.

Mix gelatin, ¼ cup sugar, water, lemon juice, and salt in a saucepan. Cook and stir over low heat till the gelatin dissolves. Add to the berries; stir well and chill until the mixture begins to thicken. Beat until stiff and fold in the 2 egg whites. Pour into the pie shell. Garnish with the berries. Chill. Serves 8.

NUTRITIONAL INFORMATION			
Calories	206	Sat. Fat (grams)	3.0 g
Total Fat	7 g	Cholesterol (mg)	7 mg
% Fat	30	Sodium (mg)	138 mg

Above figures based on per serving basis.

APPLE CRISP

4 c. sliced, pared tart
   apples (about 4 to 5
   medium)
½ c. brown sugar,
   packed
½ c. flour
½ c. oatmeal
¾ to 1 tsp. cinnamon
3½ Tbsp. margarine
¼ tsp. salt (if desired)

Heat oven to 375°. Spray square 8x8x2 inch pan with nonstick vegetable spray. Place apple slices in pan. Mix remaining ingredients with fingers until the mixture is thoroughly moistened. Sprinkle over apples. Bake for 30 to 40 minutes, or until apples are tender and topping is golden brown. Serve warm and, if desired, with milk. Serves 6 to 8.

NUTRITIONAL INFORMATION			
Calories	179	Sat. Fat (grams)	1.0 g
Total Fat	6 g	Cholesterol (mg)	0 mg
% Fat	30	Sodium (mg)	147 mg

Above figures based on per serving basis.

AUTUMN PUMPKIN PUDDING

1 c. pumpkin puree
1 c. evaporated skim
  milk
1 egg
1 egg white
½ c. apple butter
1 tsp. vanilla
½ tsp. cinnamon

Heat milk until hot (not boiling). Mix pumpkin, egg, egg white, apple butter, vanilla, and cinnamon. Add milk and mix well. Pour mixture into baking dish. Bake until firm. Bake at 350° for 25 to 30 minutes. Makes 6 (½ cup) servings.

NUTRITIONAL INFORMATION

Calories	108	Sat. Fat (grams)	0.3 g
Total Fat	1 g	Cholesterol (mg)	37 mg
% Fat	9	Sodium (mg)	71 mg

Above figures based on per serving basis.

BERRY YOGURT PARFAIT

2 c. plain lowfat yogurt
½ c. sugar
2 tsp. lemon rind, grated
1 c. fresh blueberries,
  strawberries or
  raspberries
3 Tbsp. sugar
2 Tbsp. pecans, chopped
2 Tbsp. dry oatmeal
  flakes

Wash and drain berries. Sprinkle 3 tablespoons sugar over berries and set aside. In a medium bowl, combine yogurt, lemon rind, and ½ cup sugar. In each parfait glass, layer ¼ cup berries, then ¼ cup yogurt, alternating. Chill. Under broiler, lightly brown oats and pecans. Before serving, sprinkle each parfait with 2 teaspoons of oat-pecan topping. Serves 6.

NUTRITIONAL INFORMATION

Calories	163	Sat. Fat (grams)	0.8 g
Total Fat	3 g	Cholesterol (mg)	7 mg
% Fat	15	Sodium (mg)	52 mg

Above figures based on per serving basis.

BROWNIE PUDDING

1 c. sifted flour
¾ c. sugar
2 Tbsp. cocoa
2 tsp. baking powder
½ tsp. salt
½ c. skim milk
2 Tbsp. corn oil
1 tsp. vanilla
⅔ c. chopped nuts
¾ c. brown sugar
¼ c. cocoa
1¾ c. hot water

Sift together flour, sugar, 2 tablespoons cocoa, baking powder, and salt in large mixing bowl. Add milk, oil, and vanilla, mixing till smooth. Stir in nuts and pour into a greased 8 inch square baking pan or 9 inch pie pan.

Combine the brown sugar, ¼ cup cocoa, and hot water. Pour over the batter. Bake for 40 minutes at 350°. Cool completely and refrigerate.

This makes a pudding type layer on bottom. Unusual but good. May be topped with ice milk. Serves 9.

NUTRITIONAL INFORMATION

Calories	259	Sat. Fat (grams)	1.2 g
Total Fat	9 g	Cholesterol (mg)	0 mg
% Fat	30	Sodium (mg)	241 mg

Above figures based on per serving basis.

CARAMEL BOTTOM CUSTARD

¼ c. sugar
⅛ c. water
1 (12 oz.) can
    evaporated skim milk
1 c. skim milk
¾ c. pasteurized egg
    substitute
½ c. sugar
⅛ tsp. salt
1 tsp. vanilla
Nutmeg

In heavy saucepan, place sugar and water. Cook on low heat, without stirring, until sugar has melted and turned a light golden color. Pour immediately into bottom of glass baking dish. Let cool.

Combine milk in medium saucepan and heat till bubbles form around edges. Combine eggs, sugar, salt, and vanilla. Pour milk slowly into egg mixture, beating continuously to keep smooth. Pour into baking dish. Set in large pan 1 inch deep with water. Sprinkle with nutmeg. Bake at 350° for about 1½ hours till knife inserted in center comes out clean. Serves 8.

NUTRITIONAL INFORMATION

Calories	141	Sat. Fat (grams)	0 g
Total Fat	1 g	Cholesterol (mg)	3 mg
% Fat	6	Sodium (mg)	146 mg

Above figures based on per serving basis.

CHERRY WINKS

2 Tbsp. skim milk
⅓ c. corn oil
½ c. sugar
1 tsp. vanilla
1 tsp. grated lemon peel
  (optional)
2 egg whites
1 c. all-purpose flour
½ tsp. baking powder
¼ tsp. soda
¼ tsp. salt
½ c. raisins
1½ c. oat bran flakes
Candied cherries

Cream milk, oil, sugar, and vanilla. Add egg whites and lemon peel. Stir flour, baking powder, soda, and salt together. Add to first mixture, stirring in raisins.

Roll a teaspoonful of cookie dough in crushed oat bran flakes. Place on greased cookie sheet and top each cookie with half a candied cherry. Bake at 400° for 12 minutes. Makes 2 dozen cookies.

NUTRITIONAL INFORMATION		
Calories....................92	Sat. Fat (grams).......0.4 g	
Total Fat....................3 g	Cholesterol (mg).........0 mg	
% Fat 30	Sodium (mg) ....78 mg	

Above figures based on per serving basis.

FLORIDA FRUIT WHIP

3 egg whites
Pinch of salt
½ tsp. cream of tartar
1 Tbsp. sugar
2 Tbsp. Sprinkle Sweet
  or Sugar Twin
  (granulated sugar
  replacement)
1 ripe medium size fresh
  mango, pared and
  mashed
2 tsp. lemon juice
½ banana, cubed
2 tsp. grated lemon rind
1 tsp. sugar

Beat egg whites with salt until foamy; add the cream of tartar and continue to beat until firm peaks form. Add sugar gradually, then *fold* in the sugar replacement. With a rubber spatula, *fold* in the mango. Sprinkle lemon juice over the banana and fold into the mango mixture together with the grated lemon rind. Turn into a greased and lightly sugared souffle or ovenware baking dish. Bake in a preheated 350° oven for 30 minutes until puffed and firm to touch. Serve at once. Serves 6.

NUTRITIONAL INFORMATION		
Calories....................55	Sat. Fat (grams).........0 g	
Total Fat......less than 1 g	Cholesterol (mg).........0 mg	
% Fat 2	Sodium (mg) ....29 mg	

Above figures based on per serving basis.

FROZEN FRUIT DESSERT

2 c. mashed ripe banana
1 (8 oz.) can
unsweetened crushed
pineapple (undrained)
2 c. unsweetened apple
juice
2 Tbsp. lemon juice
1 tsp. vanilla or almond
extract

1. Combine all ingredients and pour into an 8 or 9 inch baking pan. Freeze mixture until almost firm.
2. Spoon mixture into a large mixing bowl and beat with an electric mixer until smooth and creamy.
3. Spoon mixture back into pan and freeze until firm. Spoon into serving dishes to serve. Makes 10 (½ cup) servings.

NUTRITIONAL INFORMATION

Calories	79	Sat. Fat (grams)	0 g
Total Fat	less than 1 g	Cholesterol (mg)	0 mg
% Fat	3	Sodium (mg)	4 mg

Above figures based on per serving basis.

FRESH FRUIT WITH LEMON CURD

1 c. water, divided
⅓ c. sugar
2 Tbsp. grated lemon
rind
2 Tbsp. plus 2 tsp.
lemon juice
Pinch of salt
1 Tbsp. cornstarch
1 tsp. reduced-calorie
margarine
2 eggs
Fresh strawberry
(optional)
Assorted fresh fruit

Combine ¾ cup water, sugar, lemon rind, lemon juice, and salt in a saucepan; bring to a boil. Dissolve cornstarch in remaining ¼ cup water; add to lemon mixture, stirring constantly. Add margarine; cook over medium heat, stirring constantly, until smooth.

Beat eggs well. Gradually stir about ¼ of hot mixture into eggs; add to remaining hot mixture, stirring constantly. Bring to a boil over medium heat; boil for 1 minute, stirring constantly. Cool completely. Cover and chill. Garnish with a fresh strawberry if desired. Serve with assorted fresh fruit. Makes 10 (2 tablespoon) servings.

NUTRITIONAL INFORMATION

Calories	48	Sat. Fat (grams)	0.4 g
Total Fat	1 g	Cholesterol (mg)	43 mg
% Fat	23	Sodium (mg)	15 mg

Above figures based on per serving basis.

FRUIT COBBLER

2 to 3 c. stewed fruit
(apples, peaches,
berries, cherries)
1 c. cooking water from
fruit
1¼ c. whole wheat
pastry flour
1⅓ c. milk
¾ c. honey or less to
taste
¼ c. butter
2 Tbsp. cornstarch
1 egg
2½ tsp. baking powder
2 tsp. vanilla
¼ tsp. cinnamon
¼ tsp. ground allspice

Butter an 11x7 inch baking dish. Mix water, ½ cup honey, 1 teaspoon vanilla, spices, and cornstarch until smooth. Pour over fruit in baking dish. Mix flour and baking powder together. Beat egg, milk, 1 teaspoon vanilla, ¼ cup honey, and butter. Add flour and mix well. Pour over fruit. Bake for 30 to 45 minutes at 350°. Serves 12.

NUTRITIONAL INFORMATION			
Calories	243	Sat. Fat (grams)	3.1 g
Total Fat	5 g	Cholesterol (mg)	32 mg
% Fat	19	Sodium (mg)	162 mg

Above figures based on per serving basis.

FRUIT PUDDING

2 c. cranberry juice
cocktail
2 Tbsp. reduced-calorie
red raspberry preserves
1 Tbsp. granulated sugar
2 Tbsp. instant tapioca
1½ c. quartered, hulled
strawberries
Whipped topping to
garnish

Combine cranberry juice, preserves, and sugar in double boiler; bring to a boil. Stir in tapioca. Place pan over hot water; cook for 20 minutes, stirring until mixture thickens. Remove from heat; stir in strawberries. Pour into stemmed glasses. Garnish with whipped topping. Serves 6.

NUTRITIONAL INFORMATION			
Calories	91	Sat. Fat (grams)	0 g
Total Fat	less than 1 g	Cholesterol (mg)	0 mg
% Fat	3	Sodium (mg)	4 mg

Above figures based on per serving basis.

FUDGE PILLOWS

Pastry:
1½ c. oleo
   (Fleischmann's diet)
4½ c. flour
9 Tbsp. water
3 tsp. vanilla
Filling:
4½ c. powdered sugar
¾ c. cocoa
¼ c. skim milk
1 (8 oz.) pkg. lowfat
   cream cheese

Cut oleo into flour until mixture resembles coarse crumbs. Sprinkle in water and vanilla.

Cream filling well. Roll out pastry, part at a time; cut in about 6x6 inch squares. Put about a heaping tablespoon of filling on half and turn over other half and seal edges securely. Place on an ungreased cookie sheet. Bake at 350° for about 15 minutes or until light golden brown. Makes about 24 pillows.

NUTRITIONAL INFORMATION			
Calories	252	Sat. Fat (grams)	2.2 g
Total Fat	8 g	Cholesterol (mg)	5 mg
% Fat	27	Sodium (mg)	81 mg

Above figures based on per serving basis.

HONEYED PEAR PARFAIT

2 very ripe small pears,
   cored, pared, and
   diced
1 tsp. lemon juice
1 tsp. honey
Dash of ground
   cinnamon
1 c. plain lowfat yogurt
1 tsp. vanilla extract
2 graham crackers (2½
   inches square), crushed

Chill 2 parfait glasses. In small bowl, combine pears, lemon juice, honey, and cinnamon; cover and refrigerate until chilled. In another small bowl, combine yogurt and vanilla; cover and refrigerate until chilled.

To serve, spoon ¼ of fruit mixture into each chilled glass and top with ¼ of yogurt mixture; repeat layers with remaining fruit and yogurt mixture. Sprinkle each parfait with half of the graham cracker crumbs. Serves 2.

NUTRITIONAL INFORMATION			
Calories	193	Sat. Fat (grams)	1.2 g
Total Fat	3 g	Cholesterol (mg)	10 mg
% Fat	12	Sodium (mg)	117 mg

Above figures based on per serving basis.

MINT FRUIT CUP

2 Tbsp. water
2 Tbsp. sugar
5 fresh mint leaves
1 c. fresh pineapple
   chunks
1 c. sliced fresh
   strawberries
Fresh mint leaves

Combine water and sugar in a small nonaluminum saucepan; bring to a boil. Reduce heat and simmer until sugar dissolves. Stir in 5 mint leaves. Remove from heat; set aside. Combine pineapple and reserved sugar mixture in a small bowl. Cover and chill for 1 to 2 hours to blend flavors. Add strawberries to pineapple mixture, tossing to coat. Garnish with mint leaves. Serves 4.

NUTRITIONAL INFORMATION

Calories	56	Sat. Fat (grams)	0 g
Total Fat	less than 1 g	Cholesterol (mg)	0 mg
% Fat	5	Sodium (mg)	1 mg

Above figures based on per serving basis.

OATMEAL CHERRY APPLE CRISP

1 c. regular oats
   (uncooked)
1 c. all-purpose flour
1 c. firmly packed brown
   sugar
⅓ c. liquid margarine
1 (16 oz.) can sour red
   cherries, drained
2 apples, peeled and
   chopped
1½ Tbsp. quick cooking
   tapioca
½ c. apple juice

Combine first 3 ingredients, mixing well. Stir margarine into oat mixture till it resembles coarse meal. Spoon half into a lightly greased 8 inch square baking dish.

Combine cherries, apples, tapioca, and apple juice. Let set for 15 minutes. Pour into baking dish. Top with remaining half of oatmeal mixture. Bake at 350° for 30 to 45 minutes until apples are tender and crust is crunchy.

This is not a real sweet dish. If desired, add ½ cup white sugar. Serves 9.

NUTRITIONAL INFORMATION

Calories	218	Sat. Fat (grams)	1.2 g
Total Fat	7 g	Cholesterol (mg)	0 mg
% Fat	29	Sodium (mg)	75 mg

Above figures based on per serving basis.

PEACH YOGURT ICE CREAM

1 env. unflavored gelatin
2 c. 1% lowfat milk
1 c. chopped fresh
  peaches
2½ c. fresh peach puree
1 (8 oz.) ctn. plain lowfat
  yogurt
¾ c. sugar
1 Tbsp. vanilla extract

Sprinkle gelatin over milk; let stand for 1 minute. Cook mixture over medium heat, stirring until gelatin dissolves. Remove from heat. Stir in remaining ingredients; mix well. Pour mixture into freezer can of a 1 gallon hand turned or electric freezer. Freeze according to manufacturers directions. Let ripen for 1 hour. Makes 1½ quarts, or 12 (½ cup) servings.

May substitute two 16 ounce packages of sliced frozen peaches (thawed) for fresh peaches.

NUTRITIONAL INFORMATION		
Calories..................108	Sat. Fat (grams).......0.5 g	
Total Fat....................1 g	Cholesterol (mg)..........3 mg	
% Fat........................7	Sodium (mg).............36 mg	

Above figures based on per serving basis.

THREE-BERRY SORBET

1½ c. frozen
  unsweetened
  raspberries, partially
  thawed
1½ c. frozen
  unsweetened
  blackberries, partially
  thawed
1½ c. frozen
  unsweetened
  blueberries, partially
  thawed
½ c. orange juice
¼ c. maple-flavored
  syrup, sugar, honey or
  packed brown sugar
2 Tbsp. frozen (thawed)
  apple juice concentrate
¼ tsp. vanilla

Place all ingredients in blender or food processor. Cover and blend on medium-high speed, stopping occasionally to scrape sides, until very smooth. Pour into 1-quart ice-cream freezer and freeze according to manufacturer's directions.

Or, pour into 9x5x3 inch loaf pan. Cover and freeze about 2 hours or until edges are firm but center is soft. Spoon partially frozen mixture into blender or food processor. Cover and blend on medium-high speed until smooth. Pour into pan. Cover and freeze about 3 hours or until firm. Let stand 10 minutes at room temperature before spooning into dessert dishes. Makes 4 servings.

NUTRITIONAL INFORMATION		
Calories..................170	Sat. Fat (grams)..........0 g	
Total Fat....................1 g	Cholesterol (mg).........0 mg	
% Fat........................5	Sodium (mg).............16 mg	

Above figures based on per serving basis.

PINEAPPLE SHERBET

1½ c. buttermilk
8 canned pineapple
slices with ½ c. juice
(no sugar added)
Artificial sweetener to
equal 2 Tbsp. sugar
2 tsp. vanilla extract

Combine all ingredients in blender container; process at medium speed until mixture is smooth. Pour into a freezer tray. Freeze until partially frozen. Transfer mixture to bowl and beat until smooth and creamy. Return to freezer tray. Freeze until firm. Divide evenly. Serves 4.

NUTRITIONAL INFORMATION	
Calories...............135	Sat. Fat (grams).......0.5 g
Total Fat..................1 g	Cholesterol (mg).........3 mg
% Fat.......................6	Sodium (mg)............98 mg

Above figures based on per serving basis.

PUMPKIN CUSTARD

3 eggs
1½ c. pumpkin
3 tsp. sweetener (6 pkg.)
½ tsp. salt
1 tsp. cinnamon
½ tsp. ginger
¼ tsp. cloves
2 c. skim milk
⅓ c. powdered skim milk

Put all in blender until smooth. Bake in 9 inch round Teflon pan, placed in pan of water. Bake at 350° for 45 minutes. Center still may not be firm when done. Recipe equals 3 breakfast servings of egg, milk, and fruit.

NUTRITIONAL INFORMATION	
Calories...............212	Sat. Fat (grams).......1.8 g
Total Fat..................6 g	Cholesterol (mg).....217 mg
% Fat.....................24	Sodium (mg)..........551 mg

Above figures based on per serving basis.

RASPBERRY PUDDING

½ c. margarine
¾ c. sugar
2 c. flour
4 tsp. baking powder
1 c. skim milk
4 c. raspberries

Combine first 5 ingredients as for a cake in mixer. Pour into a 13x9x2 inch pan. Cover batter with raspberries. Sprinkle 1 cup of sugar over this. Pour 2 cups of boiling water over all. Do not stir. Bake at 350° for 50 minutes. Serves 16.

NUTRITIONAL INFORMATION	
Calories...............214	Sat. Fat (grams).......1.0 g
Total Fat..................6 g	Cholesterol (mg).........0 mg
% Fat.....................25	Sodium (mg)..........197 mg

Above figures based on per serving basis.

INDEX OF RECIPES

DESERTS

Cranberry-Apricot Sauce
Fructose Sweetened

Place the cranberries, dried apricots, orange rind and orange juice in a 3 qt. saucepan and heat slowly over low heat, stirring frequently. Cranberries will burst and form juice as they cook. Should sauce become too dry add apple juice or any clear juice except lemon. (This may happen as the apricots will absorb some of the juice formed).

When cranberries are fully cooked and apricots are completely soft, add the fructose and simmer for 2-3 minutes. Taste and adjust sweetness.

1 lb. fresh or frozen cranberries
½ lb. sulfured dried apricots
Rind of one orange
Juice of one orange
1 cup fructose (more if you like your cranberry sauce very sweet)
Apple juice (or any clear juice, such as white grape juice, other than lemon juice)

Moroccan Preserved Lemons

One dozen small, thin-skinned
   organic lemons (no blemishes)
Sea salt
One wide-mouthed quart jar
   washed very clean and dipped
   into boiling water

Scrub the lemons clean. Cut a thin slice off both ends of each lemon.

Place lemon on one end and quarter it lengthwise, leaving the last inch or so uncut. Fill the cut lemon with as much salt as possible and close the lemon to reshape it. Place the lemon inside the jar. Proceed in the same manner with each lemon, placing them in the jar. The lemons will release their juice, which is good. Within a few hours the jar will fill with more lemon juice and the lemons will condense. Add more lemons as needed, enough to fill the jar to the top with lemons and lemon juice. This procedure takes about 24 hrs. Store unrefrigerated with the lid closed tightly. Once filled you may place the jar in the fridge and the lemons will preserve in their own juices for about a year.

Make sure lemons are *always* covered with juice.

Use in salads, entrees or other dishes to add fresh tasting flavor.

Harissa

Mix all ingredients in a food processor to form a thick paste.

Use as a condiment to spice up broth, soups, etc.

Will keep up to a month covered with a thin layer of olive oil.

Makes one cup

2 roasted red bell peppers seeded (preferably fresh but canned O.K.)
2 cloves garlic, peeled
1 tsp. ground coriander
1 tsp. salt
⅓ cup olive oil
1 tbl. crushed red peppers.

List of foods and terms used in our recipes

All of these items can be found at natural food stores and/or ethnic markets.

Barley flour: Flour used as an alternative to wheat.

Curry Paste: Patak's Mild Curry Paste is a very flavorful seasoning from India made from ground spices. Not to be confused with Thai curry paste.

Egg replacer: An egg substitute made from blend of starches; contains emulsifying and binding qualities. For more information go to www.ener-g.com.

Fructose: A granulated sweetener that is a natural by-product of fruit.

Ghee: Clarified butter used in Indian cooking. Ghee has a nutty flavor and keeps, refrigerated, for up to 6 months.

Mango Chutney: A traditional condiment used with Indian and Asian food.

Miso: A paste with the consistency of peanut butter made primarily from fermented soybeans. It is a mainstay of Japanese cooking and contains salt. Used as a spread or to flavor soups, miso is easily digested, loaded with B-vitamins and protein and very nutritious. Miso is a living food rich in enzymes and good bacteria to help with digestion and keep a healthy colon. **White miso** is mildest in flavor and saltiness. Keep refrigerated in an airtight container.

Rice milk: Non-dairy beverage made from rice—a good dairy substitute.

Soymilk and soy creamer: An excellent milk substitute for anyone with milk allergies. There are many various types and flavors now available. These milks and creams are made from soybeans and water. The creamier the soymilk the more fat it contains. Soy creamer has the texture and sweetness of half-and-half. We use plain White Wave Silk soy creamer, found in the refrigerated dairy case.

Spelt flour: Spelt is a non-hybrid ancient grain that is easily digestible and can be tolerated by many with wheat allergies. The flour is a great alternative for wheat-free diets—not a gluten-free diet. When substituting spelt for wheat flour in recipes, you will need to use 20-25% more flour or reduce the liquid in the recipe accordingly.

Tahini: A thick paste made from ground raw or toasted sesame seeds. It is used to flavor various dishes such as hummus or baba ganouj. Also used also in desserts and sauces, and can be used in place of eggs in certain dishes.

Tamari: Naturally fermented soy sauce with a less pungent flavor. Tamari is available wheat-free and low-sodium.

Tempeh: A fermented soy product with a nutty flavor that is pressed into a cake. Unlike tofu, tempeh is made from the whole bean, thus containing fiber as well, and is high in protein. It is popular in Asian cooking as well as vegetarian diets. There are many varieties of tempeh, some containing rice, seaweed or other grains. When marinated, tempeh will absorb the flavor of the marinade. It is also very versatile in its uses. It can be crumbled, diced, fried, boiled, baked and grilled.

Tofu: Soybean curd. Soymilk to which a coagulant has been added to curdle the milk. The whey is separated from the curds, which are then pressed into a cake. A large variety of tofu is available from soft to extra firm. Extra firm tofu is often used as a meat substitute. Softer tofu can be used as a cream cheese replacement in cheesecakes. Silken-style tofu has a very creamy texture. Contrary to belief, tofu freezes well, although after freezing the tofu is just a little tougher but still very acceptable.

Turbinado sugar: Raw sugar. Its coarse crystals have a blond color and delicate molasses flavor.

Vegan: A term defining a vegetarian diet free of all animal-derived foods.

Vegenaise: An egg-free, dairy-free mayonnaise substitute with a taste many prefer over regular mayo. Made by Follow Your Heart—for more information go to www.followyourheart.com.

Love is Kind

An act of kindness is an act of generosity. Whether the giving is material or the giving of yourself. It is born out of a heart of love. Your kindness creates for yourself and/or someone else a place where love is experienced. It is spurred on by the fullness of love within you, ignited by the desire to offer love to someone, whether that person responds or not. Kindness is its own reward. You will enjoy satisfaction.

Cooking desires to be an act of kindness. An act of love! It seeks the well-being of all who shall partake.

Approaching cooking with a kind attitude will help you decide on which recipes to choose for that certain person you are cooking for. You will want to consider their tastes and their needs. With kindness flowing from the heart, the preparation of these dishes will fill you with joy. A joy that all who eat your cooking shall taste.

Anne

Index

S

V

Vanilla pastry cream filling, 145
Vegan millet and rice croquettes, with
    shitake mushrooms, 120
Vegan rice pudding, 148
Vegan sweet potato and tofu
    enchiladas, 111
Vegan, about, 185
Vegenaise, about, 185
Vegetable salad, Asian, 55
Vegetable salad, Greek, 79
Vegetables, Mediterranean marinated, 84
Velvet cheesecake, Missy's, 155
Velvet chocolate cake, 160
Velvety sweet potato and roasted yellow
    pepper cream soup, 35

W

Wheat-free German chocolate cake,
    Rachel's, 150
White bean, Tuscan, soup, 37

Y

Yam salad, roasted, 58
Yellow pepper, roasted, and velvety sweet
    potato cream soup, 35

Z

Zucchini pineapple cake, 168

Mail Order

For additional copies of "A Muse Came to Dinner" please fill out the order from below. Make checks payable to "New Frontiers", and mail to: 1984 Old Mission Dr., Suite A-7, Solvang CA 93463. Please allow 3-4 weeks for delivery.

_____

Ship to (name)

_____

Street Address or PO Box

_____

City   State   Zip

_____

Daytime phone (area code)

_____

charge my credit card   (card number)   (exp. date - mo/year)

_____

signature

Please send_____ copies of "A Muse Came to Dinner"

at $23.95 each $_____

California residents please add $1.86 sales tax per book $_____

Shipping and handling $3.95 per book $_____

Total $_____